# EARTHMOVER
## *Wherein Constant Is Rapt*

## JIM DAVIS

Englewood, NJ

ISBN 978-1-936373-44-4

© 2013 Jim Davis. All rights reserved. No part of this publication may be reproduced or transmitted in any form or by any means, electronic or mechanical, without permission in writing from the publisher. Requests for permission to make copies of any part of this work should be e-mailed to info@unboundcontent.com.

Published in the United States by Unbound Content, LLC, Englewood, NJ.

Cover art: ©2012, Earthmover, mixed media, by Jim Davis

# EARTHMOVER

First edition 2013

*For what it's worth*

# Table of Contents

## One.

Trial .................................................................................................13
Ceremony ........................................................................................14
Early Times .....................................................................................15
When Mike Was Still Alive ..............................................................17
Haven ..............................................................................................18
One King Down ...............................................................................19
The Furnace Burps With Some Affection ........................................21
Earthmover ......................................................................................23
Thunder Theory ..............................................................................25
Contrition ........................................................................................26
Ordering Chilaquiles, Again ............................................................28
Signs ................................................................................................30
Legend .............................................................................................32
Intuit the Spade ...............................................................................34
What the Old Man Victor Said, What I Said ...................................36
Waiting Room .................................................................................38
A Circle of Stones ............................................................................40
Unearthing ......................................................................................41

## Two.

The Language of a City Changed Hands .........................................47
Marianne's Ninety-Sixth Birthday ...................................................48
What Duffy Did ...............................................................................51
The Last Tasmanian .........................................................................53
Eating a Piece of Fruit on the Patio .................................................55
Happening Upon a Golden Slipper in the Street .............................57
Statue on the Green, Near Water ....................................................58
Under the Marlboro Logo, Fluourescent .........................................60
Truck Crossing a Bridge ..................................................................62
What Was Said ................................................................................63
Now, We Stand and Wave Our Arms ..............................................64

Listen to the Lions ......................................................................66
Past Kingdoms ..........................................................................67
There Is No Such Thing as Alabaster ......................................68

# Three.

Morgan Horse Silhouette ........................................................73
Dirt Left Wet............................................................................74
Another Persuasion .................................................................75
Big Sky Country ......................................................................77
This Is How .............................................................................79
Fire in the Bread Pan ..............................................................80
Horizontal Discretion .............................................................81
Comanche ................................................................................82
Chirp, Swallow ........................................................................84
Birds on a Wire .......................................................................85
On the Back of an Alligator Postcard ....................................86
Alchemy ...................................................................................87
Stronger at the Start ................................................................88
Grackle of a Grackle................................................................89
Punctuated ...............................................................................90
Curses: Wrigleyville, Summer '07 ..........................................91
Constant ...................................................................................93
Promising Conclusion ............................................................94
At the Stop of the Moon ........................................................95
Constant Was Rapt .................................................................97

# Four.

Mad Dog's Act of Extended Departure ..............................103
Acrostic Variation .................................................................105
New Kid Tries to Fill Big Shoes...........................................106
Orchestra ...............................................................................108
Understanding the Nature of the Desert ............................109
Another Retreat ....................................................................110
Two Bears Fighting on an Alaskan Beach ..........................111

The Pigeons Lean-out and Come in Swarms..................................................112  
Waiting Out Traffic After Gas and Groceries ...............................................113  
Dig .............................................................................................................115  
Agoraphobic..............................................................................................116  
Earning Stripes in the Cellar ....................................................................117  
The Dripping Faucet.................................................................................118  
Stallion Left for Dead................................................................................120  
Semiotics of Settling .................................................................................121  
The Dance of a Wasp................................................................................123  

# Five.

Article Quick ............................................................................................127  
Mint Sauce and the Tongue of Gerald Stern...........................................129  
Hoarse.......................................................................................................130  
The Best Poem I Have Ever Written .......................................................132  
Crawl Back After ......................................................................................134  
Return to Alma Mater: Napping Behind the Library Stacks.....................136  
Defining History.......................................................................................138  
Blizzard.....................................................................................................139  
Sediment...................................................................................................140  
In a Coffee Shop in the Plaza on Weed Street ........................................141  
Golden.......................................................................................................143  
Loam .........................................................................................................144  
Concern.....................................................................................................145  
Story for a King ........................................................................................146  
Camera Obscura, Colorado......................................................................147  
Sipping Tea at the Window, Colt Crosses Yard ......................................149  

Notes ........................................................................................................153  
Acknowledgments....................................................................................155  
About the Author .....................................................................................159

*Do I contradict myself? Very well, then I contradict myself,*
*I am large, I contain multitudes.*

—Walt Whitman

*My optimism wears heavy boots and is loud.*

—Henry Rollins

One.

**EARTHMOVER**

## Trial

The horse is the machine driving exaltation.
There's kingdom come     *Are these our lives?*
amid unholy breathes     we are born
into a noisy labyrinth that will someday go
                  quiet. rain
        doves & other birds. on the table
      a bowl of broken glass
remembers fruit
                    within these new dark ages
I linger in resisting, stuck in the hay-bed
until the gravity of canvas & deep-night
questions rip sheets from my half
naked body, slumber-whipped, fat-eyed
                  balancing on the quantum blade
of double bass pedals, tongue-rings, black forest
tracings on the back of a paper coaster,
transposed into the quick of my underarm
soft skin, still me, rain dove, be still, divide
& share your quarks with the world—did I
say decay? say divvy? I must have meant to.
Whose invention was the never-ending story?
Should the kingdom simmer still
in the wake of hot-dense-expansion, I'll admit
there's dreams I am not strong enough to carry.

## JIM DAVIS

# Ceremony

It motors over itself like a midnight savage
standing in front of a canvas with a bottle of wine—
said switch-back, color eater. Pre-dawn excursion

to a coffee shop, sit and watch a dog eat and puke
cigarette butts, bottle caps, little cinnamon brains
of spit gum on the sidewalk. Before the morning

papers, reading translated Benedetti, *We've all been told
how the sunsets were … a little soiled but always beautiful.*
They say that cemetery fruit hangs low, is sweet

enough, they say, for your tea. Pick a pear, should you,
from a cemetery tree, and you'll lose a glove.
And since pears only drupe at dusk, when gloves peel

away, so too your hand will be lost—the issue then
becomes how to wipe that sick-sweet juice from your chin.
How to strain-reach up and out from the grave, wipe dirt

from that sacred stiletto, use it to cork the wine, sleep.
Kill me this way: take my pen, boil me in sunset, then
blanch me in legs of rum, gears of color, dagger dawn.

Snow will find the earth, and you will find your grip
as you walk your fingers left of mid, set the tip of that
blessed dagger between my ribs, love, press until I sing.

**EARTHMOVER**

## Early Times

Certain whiskeys beg to be sipped.
Others slugged. Quick like plaster
ripped from a wound. That's sultry

June for you, rusted over—the neighbors
moved and the rat-holes boarded, those who
chose to stay were paved in. He shut the book

on rainstorms, began carving the butternut tree.
Quiet as it is, wait for the whisper
of dead things—it's there—there's worse

than ghosts in the floorboards, out there, or up
caught in the hard plastic between kitchen tile
and halogen lamp. A small child fell in a well

and was saved. He counts his ever-blessed
fingers in the dark, and his toes, one more thing
to fiddle with, another almost-answer. Golden

summer scarabs caught between the window
screens—born to this. Bored thing, pinned
posters to the wall and wished for anarchy

with fingers crossed, meaning at the same time
*Desire* and *Loophole*. Hard missed, he never was.
Hard missing certain songs more than others.

## JIM DAVIS

Certain fog hung over the too long day. I am lying
in my hotel bed, facedown, cool breeze, tied
to the bedpost with scarves. Amber poison, you

have done me hard again. Don't write about this
she said, arranging her jewelry on the dresser in the dark.

**EARTHMOVER**

## When Mike Was Still Alive

Things were simpler: tearing up the garden, drinking from a hose.
Through the filter of the bowler glass, a lemon rind's twisted pith.

Old friends tip and snigger, spill stories of Mike
the mutt who took the Hines' retriever as an acquiescent mate.

Spearing grilled asparagus, unwinding crescent rolls dusted
with garlic powder and thyme, they reminisce as the candles flicker

into puddles of themselves. They laugh and drink, recounting
Mike fighting off the dogs of the neighborhood, should they stray

onto the lawnscape of his mate. One summer, sticky with sweat
and pink lemonade, they shouted and kicked his ribs

as he tore the throat from a terrier. That was the summer
Glenview instituted its first leash-law. That's a legacy, one said,

the only thing that big dumb dog ever did aside from shit and screw.
He's had a bigger impact than me or you! they laughed

and patted each other on the back and drank and went silent
thinking of the dead dog Mike and other friends who've died,

separately remembering a snow-white road and where it led—
one went west, to a cabin near Billings, the other stayed close to home.

You gotta go sometime, just hope your story survives, they say,
fingering the lace of the cloth, avoiding eyes, rattling

chips of ice in weeping glasses, gnawing at lamb chop gristle
tagged by grill marks, sea salt and oil, spoonfuls of mint preserve.

# JIM DAVIS

## Haven

Behind these walls, knuckles knotted begging
a window air-condition unit to behave.
Hide here for a while from what's building.
Beige comforter tacked to the sill, supported
by two chairs, build a fort. Begging for pennies
at the penny arcade. Lift your tongue, she said.
She did and found a wealth of dirty pennies.
She smiled, desperate for answers to the ever-after-
pills, for regrets unwilling to admit themselves.
Shapeless inspirations quiver and clutch the leg
of a drawing table, bound at the ankles by white cotton
braided belts of any robe. The echo of a tremor
caught in the vaulted ceiling. That pull, that suck. Stuck
there, hovering. This fleeting language, she said, you
bruised notes exhumed and licked by fire, weightless
and vacuumed into obscurity, the page, *be gone*.
And you, red-coal remnants of weekends without sleep,
be buried once more. Bang trash can lids together
like a band buried beside the machine of its making,
or within, like the milk bottle sick with memories
they were willing to be rid of—sleeves of distraction,
a mouthful of currency—all that connects her
to this unrequited happening, this cruel ever-after.
Build yourself a fortress with words, she said, I will
bring you a pillow and some soup. Live here.

**EARTHMOVER**

# One King Down

*Through one choice made all choice is gone*

Was American Hardcore the avant garde we were waiting for? Did we miss it?

After forty-five minutes on the stationary bike, I wonder after mornings sewing patches to a gas-station t-shirt. Before we discovered beer we would read of Carl Sandburg plucking guitar string on the edge of a straw mattress. He died in the shadow of a meatpacking plant with one hand in the river. We drew bars on our hands in Black Flag homage. Anxious Minor Threat disciples waiting for the others, now singing Bluegrass in the shower, listening to free-radio and cutting off their jeans. Cherry Coke and potato chips at the bottom of the bag, too small to dip. Where were we …

*absolve / your words / you cannot sweep away*

when the rain began to fall? What's collected is a product of the collector, if you have come this far, you agree. There's a vacillation of volume, intensity, technique that backbones the game plan—you'll have to trust me on this: shave your head with a straight razor, watch for moles. Bask in the alchemy of a bowling alley. There's someone stuck inside me trying to speak, ringing into would-be sleep. *This is my therapy.* What, in such an ugly village, could water all possible seeds?

That isn't it. Allow me to begin again.

Rain once more. I don't know a thing about the Wobblies, but I see new life growing from the ashes. Amateur proclivity drenched with a flash dance, floor punch, double-bass-pedal-drum-thunder. When one king falls we exist in the chaos between kings. We huddle in doorways until the new next tower rises, then's riven. The *we* is all that ever mattered. Pining for defiance, you will not know what you've missed until it's gone.

Closer now. Still wrong.

**JIM DAVIS**

It's the elements of grief that sting the most.
The presentation of something's been and now
not being. It's losing sleep
and sleeping. And waking up
to the same damn thing.

It's not what's missed, but how you miss it.
It's moving boulders over the river, wishing for stones.

**EARTHMOVER**

## The Furnace Burps With Some Affection

Creation being the son of thought. I am not
within the sort of circle that would say, that has already been
said, so I say it twice, kindly, and a third time with heat.
The first time I say it I am myself, 6 foot 2, two hundred thirty lbs.
or so, teaching geometry in my spare time, trying to stay in shape
for a concentric supplement with congruent eccentricities,
that she might not find my mind in mush. I eat an apple
and crush an empty beer can on my knee, then nap. When I wake
I say it again, this time disguised as Walt Whitman,
mulling over a section of tiger-lily and wheat grass
in the parkway of the old clapboard cottage with ivy
climbing up the wall, which must belong to Paul Cezanne,
the garden so immediate: petunias braided with daisies,
other indiscretions. Upon seeing this, I am Gustav Klimt, salivating
at the gypsy flowers—I've lost my walking stick, gained a robe
which smells like Novocain and tooth decay and water lilies
rotting on the banks of the Rheine. You will by now have noticed
that this poem is not about the burping furnace, the groaning heat,
but questions, like, How was I ever able to find my way
out of the catacomb known as the Black Forest?
I was sure I'd left my verse at the Freiburg Bahnhof
sitting on the curb with a set of French luggage, riffling through its purse
looking glassy eyed to the sky that would be night, but is dark
morning, since we woke so soon to catch the train. The verse
consumed a Danish countryside with its espresso, ate the streets
of Rome, took the head of every stagnant piece of statuary
it could find. Divine, it said, wiping its chin with satin lace,
simply divine. And when I say those words a final time,
the train tick tocking alone the tracks, through the countryside,
I breathe enough fire to light the thatched roof houses

## JIM DAVIS

of every poem in town. I climb inside them, one by one,
run my fingers over their deliberate making, tilting picture frames,
picking pears from a wicker basket. I fold the clothes
left on the line, I warm my hands at the campfire I've imagined.
There is neither limit nor witness to my end.

# Earthmover

He needed a drink to steady his hand.
Emerging from one depression to spearhead another,
he would say, slurring slightly, sinkholes in the yard
had opposites: tangible, quantifiable objects
with the exact mass of what's missing—
it would not be so easy to dismiss
the scattering passage of earth
over an old man's digging shoulder, if so.

*bone the mountains down, yearn the great machine*
*(there is not a thought born in me)*

It is hard to assume the obscure nature of early commerce,
he would say. In a pair of canvas overalls, scarred by dirt,
he would ask me to consider velvet pouches, silver coins
tossed to merchants of war in exchange for clean water.
Think of woven mats, exotic birds, art
for that matter. If only it were
so easy to fill the holes. If only there were

a way to fast-forward through the obtuse, the convoluted, rewind
so the spray of dirt would switch course, waterfall and fill
the many voids, wrap conscience like twine about itself
until constant is rapt—instead, the pursuits of a Saturday evening
are swallowed by a giant, 47 pound rooster named Rex,
staring with a single, yellow eye
from the label on a bottle of wine.

*want is not a crown reserved, dust and sand and earthen mouths*
*(that does not have death carved in it)*

## JIM DAVIS

Amid the evening's dying hours, with nothing good on TV,
I remember a day too warm for its season, a collection
of fine suits, knotted ties, an assembly facing the same direction.
I remember a man whose charge was to disturb the earth.
Lilies and daffodils, small ferns in vases. The assembly rises
as the river behind the church begins to swell, flow
confident though the forest: swift, forgotten,
and strong enough to carve rock.

## Thunder Theory

Proposed mojos pollute the world.
Tawny skin of an orange nailed to a cross-
beam, pits of plums and cherry stems plastered

to a garden statue, sick with rain, heavy mushroom-
clouded heat lighting caught in a jar
with a sprig of clover and a handful of fire

ants. Ballpoint pen nubbed from poking holes.
If you have time to explain yourself, you are not
a tornado chaser, the son of a poet, or a man-

sized version of your dreams. Turnips bled
for bitter juice. Tar yourself with chicken
feather and call yourself the world.

When at last the voice between Egyptian sheets
is laced, sad-desire finds itself at your prediction: air-
guitared, hung from wires to fret over impending

chorus – climb to coda, promenade – the voice
will be the one before us, nailing skins to bay the gods.
Phenomenology, you invented formalism, blistered

under silver umbrella stands retarding rain, hot tar.
Scalp massage. Everything black, then not. Gods
abruptly stirred pounding hammers for themselves.

# JIM DAVIS

## Contrition

Sack full of photographs, I left the world
for a sandwich of gruyere and pickled onion.

I left the world one magnolia
afternoon, after Sacred Heart
butchered Sweeney Todd at Berger park,
slipped through the perfume of Louisiana
Chicken, warm dogwood dusk on the brink.

Small spring squirrels bounced, their bones
under loose gray coats—biscuit debris, honey
packets, napkins. I left the world one
drumstick, cab fare in quarters. Mufflers spoke
of Chicago in tire irons, potholes, straight

razor demonics. Outdoor singing thins
and loosens choral sonics and the small professor's
sonnets are a rooster on the block. Better terse
than self-promoted. How forgivable departure
is repaired, Oh Winter, you drank yourself to death

under the music of a tree spider, spinning after
flicked from my lapel as bluebells open gray
and green and I just don't want you
up my nose. The smell of pickled onion,
gruyere is enough to grab the city at her highest

and fling her in the lake, only for the sake
of remembering her kindly. I want your nostalgia

## EARTHMOVER

to snap over my shin. I want to begin with leaving
and an outdoor performance, finish far better: Louisiana
Chicken in a sticky corner booth, one halogen lamp,

thin and lambent, coloring the bones of this with honey.

## JIM DAVIS

## Ordering Chilaquiles, Again

A group of bobbing pigeons at a puddle whisper
nothings to the teachers picketing the Chicago Public
School system. Everyone, it seems, has a raw deal.
The elevated train struck a stray dog, which delayed the day-

trips of picketers off their picket watch. 10:15 am, nearly
and I am ordering chilaquiles again, café con leche.
The day is relaxing at the sun's insistence. Rosh Hashana.
Early fall. Some schools close to celebrate the holiday,

others still from striking, as the pigeons aptly note.
Two men in reflective vests walk the track with hooked poles
for vestigial obstructions—a tail, hind legs—I'm still waiting
for my food, and for The Savage Detectives to reveal themselves.

Finally, fried tortilla pieces, sunny eggs, strips of chicken, salsa verde.
A table of would-be students orders an assortment of sugary things
and the noon-shift wait-staff files from the bus in a line.
The chilaquiles again are fine. The coffee is hot and the sun

and did I mention I am being followed? A man whose buzz cut
reveals a map of rear skull scars, tight gray t-shirt, and stubby,
muscular, tattooed arms, is trying not to look this way. If only I could
remember what I've done, perhaps I could end this, sever the tail

and convince him (who is the tangential appendage of 'they')
to sit and drink in the shadow of the train. Want for recollection,
I will instead out-wait him, let him expose himself
as the man who stayed too long in one place. Empty

cup of coffee, empty plate and language has failed me,
and the woman beside me farts ketchup onto her fiancé's French fries

## EARTHMOVER

while he is in the bathroom pissing on the seat. She loves him, clearly.
                                                      Shake of train.

They say if you write one poem per day for forty years, you'll find
there might be nothing left to say. Worth the risk? We'll see. Until then
I'll pray to every blade of grass, touch and dwell in sequential leaves.
Simple is better, they say, though we know it far simpler said.

One of the boys who should be in school says, Have you had any head
injuries? I have, I've been hit in the head with a gold club. They used staples.
Have you read *Self-Portrait in a Convex Mirror?* It's as easy as he gets,
which is to say, uneasy as a shipdeck, hardly fathomable, upon which

those inclined to teach, teach, and those who don't
study the specifics of myofascial release, coach yoga,
and eat chilaquiles on a Monday afternoon, eliminating tails
with a shotgun in back alleys of wharf-towns, where everything stinks

like sea-foam, salt, and decay, and all good dogs stray
safely, picking bones, licking plates, napping in the never-ending sun
from this, my only perspective—*nonsensical delusions*—as pigeons,
bemused and hushing, tuck into their wings for the winter—*don't stop me
once I'm going*—all of us humming subtleties for warmth.

# JIM DAVIS

## Signs

When a dove takes to air above the yard
from fencepost to the slicing lip of gable
at the edge of the garage, above the rain
gutter, where a rising stem prospers like a river
rising from the filth of an untouched canal,

the signs begin to align themselves.
PEDDLING, one says, though the ring
and strike have faded into a faint rose,
echo of denial—another victim
of rain's impartial corrosion.

And then the broken language
of a tall thin sign like a matchstick
that reads, on three separate lines,
SPACE/AVAIL/ABLE—
swollen with unintentional inspiration.

Warnings, it seems, more frequently
than not: NO SWIMMING appears in the bay
of sharks, or after rain has spilled the sewer
channel, filling with bacteria, the bay.
And then the capital guilt, HE DIED FOR YOU.

I imagine a younger version of myself—now
nearly gone. And a vision of my father
playing softball under the lights at the park near the lake.
Then a vision of my father at the loading dock, hammering
a fencepost into a brace. My father shuffling to bed.

For me, he died? What's the intention of projected culpability?
Moreover, what bridges were built in my name, specifically?
It makes you wonder about the ones who go on pointing.

## EARTHMOVER

Although, I admit, pretention works both ways. Besides,
there is hope, not in the eyes, but in the hands of a beggar,

a withered stave that reads, WILL WORK FOR FOOD—
not one of us is any different, so long as we are alive.
And when the dove takes to air, lifts lightly onto the roof
to bustle and bob and coo beside another speckled dove,
the cordage of signs, the line of familiar imposition, unfurls.

Calmer now, I curl in the empty pockets of opportunity,
like wood lice in a palm, moving single mindedly to the next
dark patch of earth, terrified of a life without direction,
surprised by the shadow of a low hungry dove.

## JIM DAVIS

# Legend

Attached to the paradox of puissance
the Clydesdale rears and clomps
before he can admit
the picnic tables and benches
are pines and elms again.

The tears of a Clydesdale fall in rivers
he was brought to but from he seldom drinks.
Victor, what good is it to be a hero
if you have never saved someone
from pity, that tarnishing, or if you have never been seen

in the act of heroics—and if so, can you be called
salvation? doesn't the condition lie in observation?
One leg risen means the rider was wounded in battle.
A horse with one leg down would have to be drawn,
given the limits of sculpture.

Four legs grounded means he escaped without a scratch
and two encodes a noble death, although,
despite coincidental exceptions, none of this is true.
A big thick American-Italian sits sidesaddle
on a park bench, feeding ducks with crusts of bread.

Now and then he plucks the cigar from his teeth
and grins like he's heard his own valiant biography.
There's a tattoo on his arm of a warhorse charging.
Let's go back again and assume the horse
was paying attention—they say you cannot keep a ghost-

## EARTHMOVER

horse down, they rise on rear hooves and whinny
with the turning of a wave, forever in the green and gray
of city-park statuary. Where the water, in this case, is blue.
And Victor, sipping bathtub booze from a ladle
in the incandescent loft, in defense

of the morbid nondescript—personal abstraction
will have to be enough, should be only what it is
until there's something more specific to be said.
You cannot be both strong and inviting. How many hay bales
will it take to build a pyre, in the future, will you jump?

## JIM DAVIS

## Intuit the Spade

The snow whispers its ghostwriting to the frozen road.
Absently, I drift into another lane
until I am so far over that I've made it, only now
can I assume there were no other cars.
I apologize for greeting you
in a manner so terse, what I mean to say is
I apologize for being forgettable and soft.
What was the word? Predictable? Even now
the youth in Nairobi and the rich in Nairobi
are moving against the flow of bodies on the sidewalk.
The light-skinned cement mixer pleads his case
for textiles, to the nation, and assures the public
that we can sell everything. Another way of saying
everything is for sale. In 2050
they predict that Lagos will rise to a world power:
two hundred fifteen million strong. Can you imagine?
Of course, you saw it coming all along.

Once we found a dead raccoon on the road,
touched by our high beams and bloated.
In the backseat, a couple canoodled
in the manner they believed apposite.
Upon seeing this, you walk into the blustery street
and scream to the frozen road and bundled bodies,
*Who among you would wait in the cold,*
*hands still wet from the washbasin,*
*dust the snow from the face of the buried?*
I tell ya, I never saw that one coming.
You were great like that. I suppose
it all comes down to how one intuits the spade.

## EARTHMOVER

I like to think it turns soil and cuts roots,
it's face determined by clay or sand;
you, on the other hand, use it to chip ice.
Together, we use it to push a raccoon carcass
into a hole, which it dug.

# JIM DAVIS

## What the Old Man Victor Said, What I Said

Did you know DiMaggio's father
was sent to the internment camp?
Didn't think so. You a teacher?

Figures. What's new in education
is we create new hates. You weren't here
when the gangs were here, when those Poles were here—
*no man's land*, they called it, in the places where it was
and even in the places where it ain't.

Sipping again, slowly, he says,
You know what Studs Terkel told me? He said
simply, Don't let what you know die with you.

I know the wind is chasing me through trees
of orange and green over halos of lamplight
and if another autumn song exists
tonight I don't know it.

I too am modern
I am too modern
I am modern too

How are all the happy people, are they happy?
Show me a movement and I'll show you
A group once starving to be moved—not all bad
But somewhat sheepish, like a jittering wisp
Of sperm, a collection of hunting cells, fixed
By the primordial rhythm of cells none wiser
Than those basking in the heavenly balm of neuro-
Transmitters saying, Happy, Happy, Calm. There are other ways

## **EARTHMOVER**

To say this, but I won't. This is how you have it, Chicago, do pose
With me by the chimney for a portrait, before all the brandy
Has been spit upon the fire. Inspire me with foreign tongue
And local whisper. How are all the happy people, come thee hither?
Here upon the crowning roof where the gilded rooster spins
The direction of the wind, lays not eggs but position? And if there was
A plane crashed on the border, we'd be buried alive with a fireside view
Of all those men in suspenders and hoses. In the side chapel they rise

Together, sit together. A spotted dog drinks from a puddle and laughs.
I wonder always if there's anything unwilling to be saved.

## JIM DAVIS

## Waiting Room

The needle falls on 9:00 am when the man begins
to write with sound, as anyone might, with his sole
stimulus, the hum of lights, the curved complexity of spine

and skull, hanging bones, the topographical map of man's
anatomy pinned to the wall. He clicks the back end of a pen
and hovers above the page. Which element of salt turns ice

to water? he wonders to the pad. Square, an uninspired crystal.
And there's plenty of it out there, clearing the drive. Two old
women from the Philippines, he thinks, maybe Japanese—

with receding hairlines, he notes, newly conscious of his own—
engage in rehabilitation: scapular reduction, external rotation
while stretching a red band. Snap out of it, he blinks

and tells himself, Sound—write with it. Script the tune
of the blue rays pulsing through the bones of a hand,
which has swollen to the size of a hand in a glove, bulging

around the knuckle. He was lubing the channels of poetic flux
by writing with taste in the kitchen, when something sinister
put his fist through the wall to a stud. Now he writes lefty

and has forsaken taste for sound: thud of a fist on stud, quick pop
of cracking knuckle. What fortune, it seems, to be
casted for a broken hand, to see the tentacles of light floating

from the fixtures, to recall smashing fluorescent lamps
in the gully by the tracks with childhood friends, the ghost
of light rising as long tubes popped and splintered

## EARTHMOVER

against oak trunks and birch. To see behind drywall
and into structure, to see beyond shadow to substance,
to nurse another cold, or a broken bone, to live briefly

in the waiting room, not tapping fingers to her heartbeat,
hiding his face in his hands, counting waiting room tiles,
concerned purely with his own pain, grateful for such trouble.

**JIM DAVIS**

# A Circle of Stones

polished by the current of the river.

By alluding to stones, I have disenchanted
the grave site of a goldfish. I am not responsible
for absence of culture, I hold to tight maudlin underdevelopment.
I scrub blindly at building grit, so the modifiers can send themselves
to market, clean again. I gave effective strategy a name: the slow bird
needs to start early for any hope of worm.

On the wrought iron fence of the churchyard
two crows spoke in low voices: script your methods
as methodical as possible, given the limits of crow vocabulary,
given the limits of time and space and available parking. Collect
as many resources as you can, force yourself happy.
In my dream he was staring out with wide eyes
from behind the glass of the bowl, lifting his gill cover
to breathe. He turned, swam to the top of the bowl, swam back.

The water began to fog and I haven't slept since.
I can't handle it, can't hardly be handled
without rest. You should see the notes in the margin of this page.

For example: James Tate's right mind is drowsy. He identifies
with writing through haze, good practice for dementians to come,
demons of disenchantment: mute, blurry, or buried like thunder in a fog.

If consciousness is a system of organizing the clutter of the conscience
what better way than the stark romance of writing by candle, sleepless, bobbing
over the page, struggling to describe a gingko tree, under whose fallen leaves
the new complexity of struggle is buried and adorned.

**EARTHMOVER**

# Unearthing

Back and forth with the wind and a bass-heavy remix
of an old Whitney Houston song, the serene acoustic
attempt of earphones chiming in, a swarm of gulls
harassing Canada geese recently given
the gall to return, one by one, north.

Bags caught in the expanse of trees harsh reaching
before agreeing to bud, assorted Styrofoam debris
caught in the driftwood at the banks and in the timid
roots exposed. Inspired by steel-factory runoff, wind
skimming the confused surface of a river

switching current, currents of cable circulating
the city's energy, the rubber artery
and plastic running thick beneath the quiet
pair of mallards landing, rousing rings downriver
from the boat launch, steel bridge, coal tracks overhead,

where the boats put in. Signs weathered down to little more
than their NOs, pink ghosting of prohibiting letters.
If you walk too far down the wrong path, too long along
the river's edge, you'll have to hop the fence. If only
the mallards knew about the currents coursing

beneath them, sheaths as thick as brick, they would at least
pedal faster—sheathes with the same container-content size relation
as vein to circulation. The boat upstream paddles faster
than the next boat, and the boat after that will surely be last.
You wonder if the others even matter, if disaster can be

## JIM DAVIS

the only theme flowing beneath the surface of the seen.
I am here calculating the month's expenses, adjusting
for heat when the small laugh of a small child
running along the riverbank, bubbling, outside
of herself with whimsy wakes me from the fog or foam

of mindless calculation, treading through childhood, thoughts
of a young man gone west for college in the mountains,
the belly of ski resorts and natural preserves, a former student
killed by a driver. One of them was drunk
and it doesn't matter who. None of it matters

unless all of it does. I wonder sometimes if I am still alive
in the emotional grid. On Tuesday morning, gray,
small beads left in the limbs of trees and sagging wires,
the wrong song came across the radio in the wake
of the news. That's all, I said to the morning, I am here.

Two.

**EARTHMOVER**

## The Language of a City Changed Hands

Like silk worms dangling from similar trees
in every piece of French-Hungarian literature
on the shelf. These particular threads, revisited
in a winter café, sing like Johnny Mathis, blank-
eted by familiar din and fragrance. On a similar
note, we were once at the mouth of the Rheine,
in a back alley of Strasbourg, where the dolomites
peak like snow covered paps, many years down
the line, on a different map. The fact that he has
nothing to speak of is published in a broadside
at a local reading-house, beside a fire, notes and
headshots propped on the mantle. (I am speaking
of love and war, as if it were unclear.) Out back,
the notes are corralled and limited by the pursuit
of knowledge—of course I speak of university
lawns. The stone paths that cut through campus
are fluid, like the Rheine in late summer; fixed,
like the roped off paintings, tiny rooms of the druid
museum. Rubens was there, if I recall. You
lingered near him. And the blue gentian in the garden,
by the groundskeeper is kept. The shades are drawn
to avoid the glare that expounds the salt and frost
on the windows, and the sun-blind statue riding horse-
back on the lawn. Beneath the horse, risen on two legs,
a placard is fixed to marble: gentile names, a creed
etched in copper that reads: Action grows
from expression, where language is the clock and the wind.
Somewhere, thin copper filaments lie dormant in the grass.

### JIM DAVIS

## Marianne's Ninety-Sixth Birthday

I.
        A jarful of grease leaves rings by the sink.
Eggs scramble on the flatiron. Almond coffeecake.
The hummingbirds have come and gone.

The handyman in the driveway is balding.
I notice that sort of thing, these days. From the toolbox
in the trunk, he picks up tools, puts them back.
He calls to his wife, who is running the vacuum,
so he calls louder.

He sweeps cigarette butts from the sidewalk
while smoking a cigarette. In the winter
he shovels paths and never forgets
to clear the snow from the arc of my door.

Tonight is my grandmother's ninety-sixth birthday.
She has had half of a martini and cannot remember
who I am. My father is also on the line.
Mom, that's your grandson.
*Oh, he sounds like a young man.*
He is.
*Alright, darling.*

She is falling asleep.

## EARTHMOVER

II.
        There was a hummingbird at the red trumpet
honeysuckle birdfeed, raging
as she graced the wide window. I see
from a stump, cut down in the meadow,
hidden in a bed of purple wood violets,
my cousin hunting minnows in the creek
with a butterfly net, the girls splashing
by the pier in bright tubes, skiers buzzing
past, inspiring wake, inspiring laughter
as bright tubes and young girls
rise and fall in steady rhythm.

Gravel spit in the driveway.
The men drank whiskey, soothed with a splash.
The women tipped cool wine before dinner.

I control the weather, I told him.
I know exactly what I'm doing. That was before
I jumped from the roof of the garage and doubled over
with a screw through the sole of my foot.
Give me the lighter, I said, I'll get this thing going.

From the stump, I sing and parse the days
with a perfect, fleeting view.

## JIM DAVIS

III.
        The old woman is asleep in her chair.
On the counter, the cake is down a slice.
She is dreaming of a picnic and an August morning,
staring into a field of blue, when heaven was
a gentle fleck of dust in the corner of her eye,
so clearly out of reach
that to look straight at it would prove
that perhaps it does not exist.

IV.
        Maplewood smoke escapes the kitchen.
A blue heron banks above the treeline.
Sparrows on the picket fence come finally to rest.

I want to hear the screen door groan and crack.
I want to peak my head through the banister
and find my grandmother at the griddle.

In the garden, my father on his hands and knees,
digging small holes and planting thin skeins of root,
wood violets peaking from their graves.
A cold soda can in his dirty hand,
thinking of digging and planting, and nothing else.

**EARTHMOVER**

# What Duffy Did

Duffy played the trumpet for Minnesota.
Bill once asked him to join a band. One lives
in a two-flat on Berteau, the other sleeps
with a rock in his hand. It's been a while

since he slept under the awning of S&C Electric
on Devon, with tennis rackets thwacking through
his saltiest dreams. Smell of Thome Shrimp
& Rib spring through, he says the sidewalk is not

what it used to be, as if no one's going his way.
Tacks in the junk drawer pricked. He took no news-
paper from Spain and regrets it. Nothing to remember
her by—though the brindle boxer raising its leg

reminds him of a few things. Lost now, he thinks
Montrose has a harbor, and North. Listen for gulls
and walk the other way. Give me your biggest table,
Hollywood Grill, I'll cover her with paper, pepper

the evening with solar systems—Darling, he said
sifting through tacks, I can't wait for you
to leave me—there's less room than ever
on the couch. He said Dear Quinoa Salad, fuck you

and your adjacents, before running out the back door.
Support your local Quick Stop, Berghoff is down
to $4.99 and the Admiral too's on sale. Set the steel trap
he said, shaking a paper cup, knock on the trap door,

## JIM DAVIS

copperhead, I'll suck you dry. He laughed and laughed.
Fat city, I have a bio with your name on it, he said.
I'll hand over my best scepter, he said, unhasping
the latch on his trumpet case, playing taps

on the walk to Bill's door, under the loose magnolia,
over and through hydrangeas, a spirited taps to the bell.

**EARTHMOVER**

## The Last Tasmanian

On the morning of the genocide he carved kiwis in a field.
Harbor and ships painted gold with soft morning.
When evening fell, torches lit faces like masks.
Clouds and drums and thunder.
Fire touched the crying houses
and farmers and farmer's sons.
When it ended, rolled maps stuffed in bags,
chests filled and gathered. He was grateful.

Alone. Boats pointed seaward.
As the night turned over, he sat on a log
and split the brown whiskered flesh with a knife,
sliced a section of emerald fruit, which drooled
from itself, over his wrist, to the sand.
He placed the knife tip at his teeth and let the flesh
slide between his lips. He pressed its sharp sweetness
with his tongue, assumed its juice and swallowed,

sure the final rowboat had set.
All things considered, he agrees about the suffering.
Now he does his best to keep branches off the siding
of his home. He slips shears between thorny spirits
of rose limb and snips. He pushes a cart
through grocery aisles and brings sacks of fruit
to his kitchen, where he carves kiwis on a board,
chews their sweet flesh with reverence.

From his kitchen window, a truck groans
and pulls its cargo to the curb. A silver door rises

and brown-slat fruit crates are wheeled from it.
The kitchen sways and tilts like a ship deck.
A farmer stares back at him, wheat grass limp between his teeth,
a thumb stuck behind his overall strap, assures that
*this is fresh as fruit gets!* He drops
the blade to the floor, throws the bolt on the door.

**EARTHMOVER**

## Eating a Piece of Fruit on the Patio

Emerald tree-bugs crawl along his arm, the page.
Last night dreamt of snow and stirred, not
apocalyptic plates of ice, just snow, just enough

to require the dusting of the windshield
as the car engine idled.
This late in the season, after having braved
the winter blizzard, the non-existent spring,
snow was enough.

The planet's population is expected to double
its consumption of meat by 2050, which means
we will need more saws to sink their teeth

into ripe, sap-filled tree bellies
to make room for Christian farmers to plow and sow.
Carl Sandburg said that there is nothing in the world,
only and ocean of tomorrows, a sky of tomorrows—
neglecting the corn silk, husk and tassels,

the violent percussion of shotguns in the distance, muted
like the wood wind freight horn of the prairie.
Anyhow, we now need more men to make saws,

more mouths to be fed by meat, more grain to feed
the meat we will consume.
And if you think Midwesterners took to the harvest

## JIM DAVIS

you should see China, who can barely feed its pigs.
Apropos, in Chinese zodiac the year of the pig

is the year of fecundity, virility, and fruitfulness.
He sets a banana peel on the table like a squid—
golden, mottled, still.

**EARTHMOVER**

## Happening Upon a Golden Slipper in the Street

The slipper hanging from a tree branch is not a symbol.

Someone stumbled across a single shoe
and hung it from an empty limb. I took a picture

one day of it hanging, sunlight on the laces just so.
And now, untouched by human hand, it lies in the gutter,

many feet from its perch. A woman stares from her porch.
She fills her lungs with cigarette smoke, flicks the filter

to the street, where it reconnects with the filters of its pack.
A man in a straight brim baseball cap sweeps

garbage into the mouth of an industrial dustpan.
The slipper survived the winter though it fell

into blizzard snow, which grew once the sidewalks were plowed.
There are so many, on days like today, who do so little.

As the weather brightened and the moods of the city thawed,
the slipper rode the great back of the snowdrift

to the gutter, where it now rests alongside cigarettes
and papers and dog turds, once frozen in the strata of snow.

Even in the absence of symbolism, I am in awe
of these objects lying bluntly in the damp graveyard

of metaphor and purpose, how items so insignificant
in the eyes of their creator, could be so moved.

## JIM DAVIS

## Statue on the Green, Near Water

I trace slim channels with reverence,
the immortal message carved into its base,
gray-green flags frozen mid-
wave. In the wake of the debate, the crowds
thrown bones with gristle, to keep from chewing
through the chains, through the wire that wraps the roast.
Speaking of protest, speaking of open resistance they drum
on upturned paint buckets: they been there, they done it.
It's all visible from the station-platform, behind
the yellow caution line, dogs with wire muzzles
click claws and snarl at huddled derelicts.
We understand that business in the bathhouse is limiting,
is derisive scribbling in newspaper margins,
is ripped jagged from the whole.
The masses spill, the crowd on the green
is hidden, temporarily lost to steel and skin.
Everyone naked, every suitcase empty.
The cutgrass perfumes while the harbor,
so inclined, rings with swaying buoys, struck
by the clean-sweet smell of lakewater,
the boat sides gently tapping. The traffic at the launch
is concerned only with whomever was left, the shapeless
figure, given shape in guilty subconscious,
to receive the gray-green hand, straining backward,
the rider screams *Assumption* as his horse kicks
on two legs. Stretch the saddle, dig deep in the stirrups,
tip cap and sip from a canteen as we
chase the scene between mouthfuls of bone

## EARTHMOVER

and gristle, grease dripping from our chins.
The drumming has stopped, the buckets carried away,
the rider painted with flame in the orange day,
his calls drowned by traffic
in the rocking, indifferent harbor.

## JIM DAVIS

## Under the Marlboro Logo, Fluorescent
*for Tony Hoagland & Smoke Daddy*

I can read DaVinci's backward Latin. I think
back to the first time I wore pants without boxers, shoes
without laces, socks, guilt or worry—back to that
time I prayed the rosary, the first time I drank

Budweiser at the smokehouse, standup
bass thumping to blues as Detroit went up
14-10 on Green Bay. Pink threads of pulled pork, burnt
ends on a butter-roll, toasted, pickles and Tony

refers to the world as a wild cascade of data,
disparate stimuli in desperate need
of a meal, a glass of water, humble arrangement.
Under the arm of a beautiful, sweaty girl, her pink

yoga mat, trundled, as she waits for her pick-up order.
Three or four pairs of hands clap when Green
Bay regains the lead. Lights have been left on in rooms
across the way, which doesn't mean anyone's home –

syllabic value affected by time, as after all, we find
there still is night. The singer belts a high-pitch
Jeff Buckley warble, creamy falsettos enhance Tony's
Narcissism, what exactly it means to us both. The barback

is wrapped like a gift, the girl I came to meet, who
I've called the wrong name. A thing's proximity in time

## EARTHMOVER

and space is enough to confirm their relative relationship.
Green Bay extends the lead and snow begins to fall.

Did you notice the wormhole? time-lapse? Written backward
all names are ghosts. Tell me again how everything is holy.

# JIM DAVIS

## Truck Crossing a Bridge

A small portion of me is haunted, at least
the gray matter has grown thin
roots like ivy climbing along the brick partition
between the grout-creases of a crumbling bridge
in a quiet stretch of forest, rattling chains
down a long corridor, vibrating with the violence
of eighteen wheel trucks. Lying in bed
as a child, on the top bunk, and I tell you,
I don't know how I remember, but
a truck rumbled over a bridge somewhere:
that was the explanation they gave, the standard
response to a shook earth. I dropped
from the bunk and filled a glass at the tap.
A white tail deer passed the window,
grazing on tulips, was gated, corralled by
wrought iron fencing, which lines the steeple shadow,
a long black stripe on the forest floor. The buck speaks
in a language with which I am no longer familiar.
I'm telling you, some days I just don't know
what the hell is going on in here. Trip the river,
skip stones across it. The palms shake
with every exhale, and who knows how much of this,
due to the countless collisions I've incurred, I will remember.
Shake it off, you say, we're only here.

**EARTHMOVER**

# What Was Said

Outside it's raining.
Within, I encourage paint to flake from bruised walls
like birch bark, like letters from camp to home.

This is the way the going gets
when the track has soured, when we turn to scratch
off tickets for the rent. To say the least, we are here.

Of course we were laid together,
Salman Rushdie tucked us in. I never heard
of this guy before tonight, but he can weave
a bedtime story for the insomniac among us. Salman says,
Here's a handful of pills, chase them with beer.
Fat drops attack the sill. Just as I lull
into hard pillow sleep, I remember what was whispered
on a dry winter evening such as this, weeks before
our rendezvous came to an end.
I will begin my hermitage at daybreak.
& here's Venus breaching the blinds at dawn.
I'm stiff. Movement—isn't that the whole story?
Take and concrete me: complete my stagnation.
Make me not want to write anymore.

A gospel choir hangs
from the apartment windows, yawning
in precipitant threat.
Everything now is gray.
Darling, you warned me:
once the cows take their sides
there always next comes rain.

## JIM DAVIS

## Now, We Stand and Wave our Arms

The market has closed for the morning.
We share the afternoon
with a French press, divided
between chipped porcelain mugs.
Next, we stand against
the stern of a ship and wave our arms
at another ship as it rolls backward on the horizon.
Sails clap like sheets on a line.
Barking gulls. A coiled rope
and notches carved in the mast for days.
An army of barrels with French
stamped to their sides. Feathers drop
to the depths of the engine room,
where smoke escapes
and gears struggle to turn.
We are thrown by waves
and as the boat flips

one hundred years have passed.
The keel arches, its belly a ribcage
buried in the sand, bleached by wind.
We wonder what the barrels held.
What again with the coiled rope?
Fathoms deep. Nets full of fish
that will not be pulled to deck
nor market. It seems as though
we are always sitting here
in the corner booth of the coffee shop
after a night of drinking.

## EARTHMOVER

The plunger has been pressed:
amber & almond, warm & breathing.
Gulls circle to their unseen boundary,
turn to shore, perch in the palms,
and atop the arching keel.
You notice something
far off on the horizon.
You stand and wave your arms.
I squint and strain to see it,
sink back into the booth.

**JIM DAVIS**

## Listen to the Lions

The enemy of the plowman is the boulder,
they say. In Ireland the stones tripped on
while turning soil are used to build walls,
to fashion partitions for grazing sheep,
so that they may continue plowing, bleating.
In Appalachia, there's a steaming machine
that chews through mountains, industry proving
too powerful for nature's colossal grace. They grind
its bones and mix mortar and cast it in long tubes,
carve it and ask it to support ceilings. And if I might
recommend one thing it would have to be …
listen to the lions—they run the world.
And, hey, nothing lasts for sure, it's all crumbling.
The tools used in restoration, the ones coating
the city with dust, will one day be dust themselves,
and we are left only with the lions. I can see
one now, his mane blooming from the collar
of a white robe, splayed across the king-
sized bed sheets in the master's quarters,
licking viscera from his quiet paw.

**EARTHMOVER**

# Past Kingdoms

Before the cadence of the morning
bus, he sits tapping small disks of cigarette ash
to the pavement, exhausting into Chicago winter
the taste of rot-gut whiskey and India Pale Ale, which was on sale
at Louie's this week, coats his tongue as he considers constellations
covered by a blanket of gray hindrance, a pocket of snow
waiting above the eminent skyline, drifting slowly down— as if
there was another way to fall. He could have finished
an entire box of wine before the Christmas party, he does not recall
stealing a sweater with bells from his mother's closet.
That was the night he met Johanna, the beautiful Swede,
who warmed his bed that winter. The sweet stench of moth balls
and brandy, eggnog and her breath, sour from cigarettes,
entered his as the wind bit through hideous reindeer and bells,
split thin wool and carved his pale chest, even less
between their lips, only the smudge of breath, a bit of English.
He dropped the filter, ground it with the toe of his boot.
Along the road, faded symbols evoke the King of Tile,
King of Carpet, the King of Mufflers & Breaks,
and the best steak sandwich in the tri-state. Who can a man trust
at this hour of day, now that leaves are dead again, once sleet has
cleansed Ashland of its rat piss and split buck and firework mortar?
Upon resumption, he looks up as the 8:19 to Cicero hisses
and pulls away. There has to be more to say about family,
about friends that fell through ice. He takes a bite of bagel
with chive spread, saves half. He taps a pack of smokes on his knee,
thinking of the many synonyms for sovereignty.

**JIM DAVIS**

# There Is No Such Thing as Alabaster

What but the wager of reflection remains

nameless, goads leaves fumbling over the road to
relevance, warm the phone on the floor with voice?
Should you doze in a pillow of your own arms

your dreams will be shapeless. Any variation
of process can be applied to late-night bars
on the shady-side of the river, where they are

free to sling drinks at the brink of frenzy. Where
porter fuels peonies and bluebells
in the garden. There has to be a permit

to touch [stubborn] the hand and [gentle] the face.
In awe of pulsing storm approaching blue, its
Paleolithic rhythm sifting vanilla

desert. Do not lose June's humble buzz
of insects, Blake's existent songs—now that
locks are frozen over, sewer caps steam like
her breathing.
One cut red onion sweating in a bag.

Desire, derived solely from lust, from dark
speckled night, from the king of speech. There is no
such thing as Alabaster, says the Dodo,
stepping off a rock into the sea.

**EARTHMOVER**

Poetry, the augured principality
of precision, of concision as it adheres
to the limits of all that's written and seen,
or sung, or hung by small thread to the bark

of a willow where the cartoon carving
of a principled existence determined
by the envy of the honeybee, who,
seeing advantage in sniffing stamen,

will repeat. One thousand times over, the red-
throated loon, crazy with boredom and desire,
whispers to her huddled brood
                      *chirp, swallow, repeat*

Three.

**EARTHMOVER**

## Morgan Horse Silhouette

The once well-pelted Morgan horse limps,
two arrows plugged into his graying shoulder,
another in the strong meat of his neck.
He is swallowed by the horizon. Sand and rock
stained where the fire was. The face of a hog,
slain and roasted, is buried.
Buried for the wolves, or the thought of wolves.
Olive brush divided by rippling canyon crust
at the lip of the drop. Two men on their knees,
praying at an altar, praying for their lives, ringing
water from stone. Cut through their camp, a stream
of trampled ground, dust still settling. Still air. Heat.
Somwehere, the Irish elk sinks into the bog.
The grizzled rogue drags his heel in the sand, growls
to boost the tension. He coughs and spits.
Clear as the sky scrubbed of cloud, you could see it coming
for miles. The rocks are weeping. The alter crumbles.
The concession of failure is free to reason.
Grouse rise from the brush as two cracks peel still air
from the face of expanding country.

**JIM DAVIS**

# Dirt Left Wet

Running from the city with water
leaking through two cupped hands.

Trading venison steaks on the river bank
is no match for alms on Sunday morning.

There ain't a culture in the world that don't
pray about something, he said.

Conifer trunks, rural Wisconsin's severed
acreage. Soft sons of bark in speed boats
drowning strung perch in gasoline.

The pole might well be limp, the minnows are
white-eyed. My father pulling cigarettes to filter
on the dock, casting long scarves of lure
for the muskie he caught one 4th of July weekend
when he was a boy. He and I stuck knives inside
the belly of what we found, no matter how good
the eating was to be. A twelve inch bullhead, heavy
with roe that spilled into our musky hands:
small planets, small occasions, worlds
to be explained away, as muskie supper
bubbled on the stove.

Lying in bed that night
I heard the campfire aching in the pit.
Until thunder came, and lightning lit the town on fire.

**EARTHMOVER**

## Another Persuasion

A trip to the art institute is worth the bus fare—
though that's not it, is it? It certainly is
not the fear of falling. Not rain. It's the sunlight
fading fast, and there's only one way to feel
confident at dusk, I haven't found it. I want to
be a specialist. I want to be a supernova, brighter
than anyone expected and cooking, forming elements
of life and seizure, inside out. Turkey Ruben, cuppa joe,
extending novelties as far as they'll go.
                         Remember *Smints*? Remember *Saved*
*by the Bell*? Have you heard of it or do you remember? The air
is becoming stale, smells like train grease and barn dust.
Time to modify my scenery.
                                 I told you I could jump
to that ledge he said, after he did. And then I did. We then
were stuck on the ledge.
                   Those who hate religion and reference crusades
are afraid they'll be converted – the conviction of good
catholics is commendable, wide-reaching, all-embracing,
and yes there are bad ones, many, making news and trouble, but
no more than the religion-less. (I have a drawer full of tasteless
birthday card.) Even art is catholic, at least the good stuff is,
or decidedly non-catholic. Nothing more than the wide-eyed
divine trying desperately to make sense of things.
    All the while I have been writing poems inside
matchbook covers. Here's the most recent, I call it Club Lucky:
                *Bye Molly!*
                *Buy Phillis.*

## JIM DAVIS

And since the human trade is nothing to joke about,
I try to stay delinquent. She is used to being stared at
so I don't look at her at all. That cannot be the way.
Days later, it still isn't.
> It's cold in the bed of imaginary lovers.
> Arthritic missionaries tend to miss opportunities.
> That said, I've met some very fine catholics.
> I only know communists by title.

There's no such thing as fear of heights, there is only the fear
of falling, which is legitimate. An important step you'll have to
note if there's any hope of understanding my work. Last night was
as important as any, though this morning was worse.

On my gravestone it will say "Undefeated at Midnight
Arm Wrestling on Hoods of Convertible Coupes"
and that will have to be enough.

**EARTHMOVER**

## Big Sky Country

How terrific the rain
        clouds must be, confederate
                gray and angry. How felt-
like the pelt of caribou, it seems, the elk like
shag carpet in winter, when run through by dry,
chapped hands. Remember to beat the jeans
like a rug, hang them over the banister's iron
lap, and slap them with a broom, or your open hand.
Cover your mouth.

How page-like the dunes appear, one large stack
turning in the wind, leafed through and falling away.
The woman on the ledge steps and pins a dune-page
as it escapes me, loose and dancing down the gritty
sidewalk. How exactly does the script read? Do I approach?
Does she? How terrible it all seems in the Big Sky wind,
spilling down from tall peaks, covering the path with leaves
and rustling; the beaver laughs as my cap tips and flies away,
two long teeth clicking at the edge of the cold creek. Beat
the jeans, I said, and roll up your sleeves.

The fire blinks yellow then red. I trace a line that seems
familiar; show up late to work, remember the man hung
by guitar strings. I put my arm around his limp shoulders
and tell him deeply of a Big Sky chorus, which I knew
was the wrong thing to say, so I went on: A rose is a plum,
which is the theory of a rose, blood petals crystallizing
with Frost in the early morning. (I think I'd rather hunt
on my hands and knees than wake up again for this.) In the garden-

## JIM DAVIS

sill at the window-lip of the stark third floor apartment, floors
lined with newsprint. I tip a green spigot and sprinkle water
over wilting hydrangeas and yellow stems. I spin the rotary
of a black-lead telephone, hold the mouth piece and speak:
Pull a chair to the open air, hold your hand out, feel the rain.

**EARTHMOVER**

## This Is How

Lose your voice yelling,
that's where you start,
then take a private plane to Eagle, Colorado
but don't sleep the night before, any more
than four hours and you'll have to
start over.

If you smoke, smoke.
Pour milk into coffee and watch
as the pale cloud rises like disturbed sand
at the bottom of a murky lake in a black forest
on the outskirts of town, settled
on an island, in the mountains, then stir,
then drink if you drink
coffee, even if you don't.

Stare into a stained mirror,
brace yourself with hands on the washbasin
and see a grizzled Bukowski staring back, not the dead
Bukowski, the dying Bukowski,
the one piss drunk in the roominghouse,
and rewrite a Robert Frost poem, people seem
to like him, and since you're out west,
surrounded by red mountains, you might
as well.

# JIM DAVIS

## Fire in the Bread Pan

allow me to say again: the bread pan / caught fire. some called out, fire! / some called rape. some grain / stored in the silo became centuries. allow me / to cauterize the garden. allow me / to bury snapdragons in salt. wound of a spade / we've done our best to intuit, four hands grasping / its stalk. the sky was right when it said, red sky at night. / morning was cold, but blue / vines continued climbing, grew stiff / days on the yellow couch, punctuated / by sleeping / and waking of the dog. / long fingers of ice at the window, strung white / lights. whisper. shake. scrape the pan / smoke hung from the rafter with prints from being touched / what we've buried, trembling outside / tucked in a blanket of dirt as it dries

**EARTHMOVER**

## Horizontal Discretion

In the shake of drunken conversation she is / overwhelmed by wonder. After / years of quiet, she thanks the folded coaster / that she and her sister are again close: childhood / preoccupations behind them. It is / no longer, who's the better swimmer? It is / no longer, what type of men will we marry? Hanging / laundry, she said, when you write / while sitting, conversation is / the only thing that sways. // When you write from a ship deck, your senses pitch / about a midpoint: horizon. / When you sleep upside down, you drown / in conscience. You'll know you have / made it when your pockets fill / with sand. Remember, as you empty / seashells and quarters on the bureau / by the bed, on any waking sea / our horizon is comprised / of thousands of points / the equidistant limits of sight / blurred by lines of heat / scripting off the bread pan fire.

JIM DAVIS

# Comanche

Comanche, lone survivor of the hour-
long battle that proved to be Custer's last, walks slowly
back to town, filthy with gunsmoke and blood spray.
When they used to say, forget you and the horse
you rode in on, they meant something different entirely.
Upon news of the death of the Achilles-Cowboy,
the women of the town tried their best to remain
normal—the difference between espresso and cappuccino,
they'd say, is a little hot air, a touch of disruption.
Ms. Mayberry raved about the sliced and sautéed
rooster combs her help prepared, a Mississippi recipe
she thinks. And when the bells of the local church rang
one of the ladies said, Big Ben, she said, is not a clock
but the thirteen ton bell of the clock within the tower
of England's House of Parliament. Facts remain, ring
truer at times. Everything needs to be said at least once
in order to assume its role as thing. For instance, today I am
sitting, elbows frozen to the faux-marble countertop of one
of our remaining bookstores, trying to find poetry
in psychology, in philosophy, and, hell, in the sins and cosins
of trigonometry. If you understand the value of your opposite
and you know your adjacent length, as well as the angle
of perspective, you can solve just about anything. Try not to
be distracted by beautiful women heralding weather
with their dresses pulled above their knees, naked feet traipsing
through puddles—only once it rains and saturation is inescapable
will they frolic, splash and kick puddles at each other, a line
of liberated women, performing an impromptu cancan through flood.
This, clearly, is not an elegy, but a celebration, however obliged
to bow their heads and courtesy as the battle-worn Comanche hooves

## EARTHMOVER

his way through town, dripping black with rain and soot. They find
themselves grateful, shaken, bubbling with prayer that they might
someday forget this horse and it's vacant saddle, touching
their chests and lips and whispering something inaudible
like divine voices, like shameful, human voices, whispering
at this image, this still mobile pillar of what was lost.

**JIM DAVIS**

## Chirp, Swallow

Swallow hard. There's residue at the back
that will not flush: sip tea; will you
boil water for the empty mugs? Their mouths
ache like crying birds in a nest of twigs
and hair. The spider is a brute,
an assassin has come to web, then die.
The sky is an empty, naked blue; pour
a finger of gin and stir add ice and to shake
would be redundant, they shake regardless.
Swallow the pills marked with today,
and stow the artillery box in the medicine chest.
Dry heaves are nothing in winter, pull harder
in fall, driving the familiar back streets
from college. To college go earnings, they rotate, you are
torn at the cuff: you, finished, early; you,
never, done; you, swallow, something
that I cannot swallow: a tea bag
in an empty porcelain gullet, a cigarette, ash.

**EARTHMOVER**

## Birds on a Wire

Let's be real for a moment,
we only get it half the time, if we're lucky.
Let's be the stubborn coat of textured ice
on the car window, warmed by vents.
There is something wrong with the treble.
The radio is trouble, I could see it
if these damned headlamps weren't broken.
If the ice didn't guide me toward the hydrant.
The ashtray smells like stale ash, as if it were
becoming dirt. I think the idea behind it all
is the romantic portrayal of one's own personality—
is that right? I've been told that
we are all, on a genetic level, 99.9% similar,
which leaves very little room to be ourselves.
These nights at the typewriter, these empty
bottles of wine, all the blue of the moon
that artists have painted and told of so many times
before, with purple tongues and teeth. Where,
in this thin sliver, will I lie? In the unmade bed?
On the flattened cushions of the couch? Where,
among the infinite consideration of stars, do I throw in?
And if we are only right half the time, I suppose
it is in the other half where we are obliged to lie.
Let's be real, we all see the crows
perched incredulously on the wire, in the cold.
We drink the song of their reductionist self-
pity, how they wait to pick our bones
as line after line of traffic slows to a stop.
Their placement like notes on a scale.
The stoic pole, their clef.

**JIM DAVIS**

## On the Back of an Alligator Postcard

Did you hear about that woman
pushed down the stairs for her phone?
Oh, golly—it's hard out there. They want it.
They go take it. The morning was white and blue.
She was always mistaken when using parenthesis
in letters—the rule, she thought
was that if punctuation closed, it was encompassed),
(if not, not.)
There was thunder in the pockets of night
where lightening once rang. No flash.
No light shed, to make blue the statue on the lawn.
Dance no longer, someone said.
I've begun to dream in letters, the postcard read,
which I heard was unfeasible—suggesting
that perhaps I do not sleep, but breathe
through a hollow reed in the wetlands of rest.
If I should die before I wake
I pray my soul takes a cab to Division Street, to drink
and screw all the nights I missed out on. We're allowed
about three billion heartbeats in a lifetime.
I would move here for good and slow down, but the beats
would keep ticking, fall like sand through the waist
of an hour glass, stalks of corn to a thresher.
Scribbled in blue ink, she says
Screw it—I'll take what I can get. Borrow time?
Sure. You can figure out my tab once I'm gone.
Everything is enclosed.
She went out dancing.
Ripe, Florida oranges fell to the dirt.

## Alchemy

This beauty is killing me; humor me, would you
Conjugate the algae? Convert nitrogen to
Something divisible by whisky. I'll handle the
Denominator, you be the numeration of sky.
Why, when we speak of alchemy, do we always turn to
Flames licking the face of your Orion Constellation?
Hunter, Jäger, Cazador, you, con-
Sistently astonished by a system of ladders and
Chutes, your one chance to insist the congregation submit
Their daily wages to pay penance for the shepherd boy,
Back after translating the desert, to speak of camels
Blinking a third eyelid in the wind, crocs the same, as they
Submerge demurely into the marsh: universal safeguard,
Suggesting that water once was sand.

## JIM DAVIS

## Stronger at the Start

Hinges like teeth, tiles tilting from residual malt
filtering through the bowels of a minor god
flipping through a notebook on the pot.
He writes. Forget me now, Dione, as if you could
possibly maintain the position of forgetting, let slip
your web of knotted sinew, of bone, of gristle
in your grip like a briar. There is a woman, naked
but for robe, then without a robe. Nothing has ever been
discovered through hair, eyelashes, or fingernails—in order
to paint what's there you'll have to see what's not, what is, and how
they trade symbioses, in gesture and sense—see her
without pretense, outside sequential logic, for she, Dione, is
beyond us, and is us, and likewise is not. Without
her, we fall without knowing, the proverbial rug is wet
with flakes of leaf and compost, yanked out from under.
When psychology is beyond cartography, he will leave
the present Venus of Urbino with her foot propped up
on a bucket, a small heating fan whirring at her back.
He loved her once and wonders now
if it's possible to fall out of love, how slow
the decent must be. Yet here he is, reading graffiti
on the inside of a bathroom stall, standing at the precipice
of a plunge the artist can hardly imagine.
Shadow, forget-me-not, blue, then shadow.
Before the writing on the wall comes to life.

**EARTHMOVER**

# Grackle of a Grackle

Something big is in the thicket near the stream, shaking
berries from their cluster, collecting twigs and hair and bone
for a colony nest. There are lessons to be had: "Do Unto
Otters," as they say. Crack shellfish on bellies
coated in oil. There is something to be said
about the amount of lead in a pencil, ink in a pen,
the motion in an ocean of conversation, frozen to ice
in the realm of empire penguin, harp, and bearded seal,
all wondering at the size of the polar bear, which happens to be
enough to break the ice, (males approach
1,500 American pounds and scrape the ceiling at 3 meters
on hind legs, rightly, 10 feet). 85% of communication
in non-verbal, so the bear's posture (in addition
to concentrating the load) would likely break
the frozen skin of aforementioned ocean, that is,
in the clumsiest presentation I can muster, the ice. Is melting
caramel for an apple the surest sign of fall? Hardly, it must be
Big Paw, when he meets the Berenstain Bears on a hillside
after breathing fire and picking teeth with oak trees
to strum something folksy on the guitar. They find him
useful for gathering nuts from the highest limbs.
Buckets with fruit of the harvest. Ah, now. Time has escaped
me—I had better consider the reader and get to the point …
But I am more concerned with naming everything
for which I tried to understand, tried to hold onto
and couldn't. For instance, the clap of a car door,
the call of a grackle, the *caw* of a grackle:
somewhere between click and quack.
Summer still covers their nests, images of youth
before the fall, when oak leaves turn and shed and the air vibrates
with a honking throng of geese on the schoolhouse lawn.

## Punctuated

Why would this be of interest unless I told you
about the man loading crates of Royal Crown
into a truck   they call him Tim    an ex-marine
whose sore back drove him to liquor     whose liver
failed him     hey    when I say *poetry* will you strip
down to your underwear     I would rather you imagine
Tims wife waiting in a nightie    touched
by soft yellow light from the streetlamp as she sits
cross-legged on their unmade bed    besides
why would you want to write    she said    wheres the good
in book reading when the power lines are down    I imagine
worlds without punctuation    I remember tearing off my fathers
arm but it grew back    itches    he said new limb branching
from his plaid jacket sleeve    I am not ashamed
to chase the things Im not yet able to explain    are many
students able to read    Can they write    Youll see with testing
that 30% of those in Chicagos Public Schools are hemorrhaging
with lack of explanation    lack of ability to explain
cannot conjugate a verb   pluralize a noun
much less evaluate the validity
of a comma,
whose presence after the period of abbreviation
as in Mr., as in Rd., i.e., e.g., etc.,
can force one into a career of loading crates onto a truck,
can cause a bad back, stress an ab to herniation,
drive a man to drink. Tim, after half a bottle of rot-gut scotch
can go on and on about the promise of progress giving way
to the value of production—how the desire to write is different
than the desire to create, says Tim,
scribbling nothings with his tongue upon the air.

**EARTHMOVER**

## Curses: Wrigleyville, Summer '07

Sitting shotgun in the paddy wagon, chatting up Sheffield drunks
while his partner perfects a three point turn, our veteran hurler
is shelled by the Bronx Bombers. What veil has been pulled over
the north-siders this time, what curse? Tree limbs stretch
in kinder weather than expected. Padraig O'Connell is offended
by the term *Paddy Wagon*. As a teen, Pardraig mugged a man
on dock road—beat the face off him, only to find pockets stuffed
with lumps of coal, an orange vial of pills for back pain. Outside
the Catholic Church, he is handed a pamphlet professing the seven steps
to find your true mind. Padraig's partner, Raymond, a Czec, has developed
a personality affected by 80s bubblegum teen movies, wrapped in the guise
of nonchalance. He's tattooed with the symbol for Maum – the mind, soul,
spirit of Korean religiosity. Allow us—they suggest to the waitress,
Amber, whose pink breasts been whipped by sun, will peel—to share.
There has to be away around this, they say, turning right into an alley.
Anyway, they say, the illusion must first be reduced. Alluding to

summer's deconstruction, the method of discovery,
should one decide to again find the way.
We were told rain. No rain.

Things here, without sleep, become strange.
Sheffield—pullulation (the effect of the pullulate)
springs with the last hickory crack.

Over the phone: so this is alone. This is alone, she said, yes.
Poetry exists in the destruction of poetry, you said. I agreed,
holding myself like a god, making rivers of urine in the alley.

## JIM DAVIS

No more holly-hocking. Less roseate mumbling.
Only a chipping sill, the Maumed safety of an afternoon
where rain, I assumed, would fall.

Blue sky, even still, has burst.
The streets are flooded
with drunks.

**EARTHMOVER**

# Constant

Alone again in my study—a word I prefer
over *office*, or *chamber*—where a guitar leans
against a bookshelf slating spines for salvation:
*Relationships and Culture*, the twelfth edition
of *Child Development*, the *Dictionary of Theories*
and a collection of DVDs in crisp polyurethane
I don't care enough to watch. The sun rising
dry on the horizon. Mid-summer. Half drunk.
Long days. Trifling sleep. The slight sting of pink
shoulders, back-of-neck, top-of-calf behind the knee—
sun struck, slightly, if only to remind myself of traded glances
between life and death. You can't say that to me, she said,
standing on a crowded street, (how I wished it was raining!).
The neighbor's Oldsmobile growls to life and a woman walks her dog
through hazy obligation. One mass—11 am—I'll miss it.
The cap is missing from the hydrant mouth and a child's
pool, stamped with Curious George chasing a beach ball,
sits stagnant below. I wish I could report a slow drip
so orbiting rings might spirit the limits of sound, exponentially
powerless as they distance themselves from origin, but no,
nothing, still—not even a breeze to trouble its skin—
so I dropped a penny in for luck on the way to my study
where I write about happenings and lack of happenings,
thoughts filtered through slivers of venetian blind, spilling dull
light into the room, shielding me from the stacked metaphor
of each brick laid in perfection. It's about the process, she reminds me.
It's about all these people and all these things giving life to one another.
It's about having what it takes to forego poetics and aim for poetry.
Before falling asleep on my keyboard again I think, perhaps hope,
that one day they will tell of it, as I continue to tell of them,
those unwilling characters, unwitting passers-by, becoming mine
as I carry their burden on tender, curious, smoldering shoulders.

## Promising Conclusion

Egret over black water stirred. Her hair
pulled tight and earlier that night
a white sundress hugged her close, calico
and sensuous, electric in the breeze,
sending her scent over hyacinth gardens,
fields of tall grass, nesting in the hill-beds.
She slips something into his palm
and curls his thick fingers into a fist.
In the other hand, his spear: cypress branch
carved to a tip, whittled and fire-hardened,
pierced through her abdomen, blood through
fingers like water through reed. She looked down
then, mercifully, into his eyes, kissed his cheek
before setting her flaming torch
to the gracious pyre beneath.

**EARTHMOVER**

## At the Stop of the Moon

Silver horn of a spoon's handle
balanced casually on the rim of a mug.
She tucks a length of hair behind her ear,
cheeks buckled, sucking at a milkshake straw.

I'd never lie to a girl who could beat me
through a burger and fries. Ask for decaf
they'll brew you a fresh pot, she said,
                            I bet they will.

They did, and many pots after, when all but morning
was more or less the same, a good thing
appeared on the cusp of the new year: two young friends
surprised by adulthood: blue light softening angles

into calm water. Lemon in the ice of the drink; seeds.
Spinach? she said, really?—put some hot sauce on it –
                          let's see how bad this can get …
Mountains and pinto beans see enough of themselves,

change face. Late at night, he shakes
the way he did the on the morning the waves distorted
belief—when the moon turned over itself, unaware
                          of its tide, the terrible pull

like a blanket above the eyes of two young lovers,
slowing the world through human concentration, shared

## JIM DAVIS

breathing—pausing between songs—then shaking
                                    until it stopped.

Baby, she said, someday you'll turn me in
to something beautiful. I'm sure of it …
There is no other way, she said.
        Then, softly, a silver spoon stirring.

**EARTHMOVER**

## Constant Was Rapt

> *Constant was rapt, imagining that the fountain was*
> —Kurt Vonnegut, Sirens of Titan

Imagine that the fountain *is*—
should anything be so certain.

Imagine potent streams firing
into the rainbow of their making.

Imagine swans cutting through mist
to land and float. Nothing has ever been

so concrete, so sure.
Now, imagine that the fountain *was*—

an object eternally available
in the brick oven of memory.

Perfume of baking bread;
musk of dry, burning leaves.

Reflect on the man leaning over
the buffer of theatre popcorn

to joke at the villain's costume
as the chords tense on screen.

Picture a girl with pigtails
laughing at the discomfort

## JIM DAVIS

of her brother's broken ankle
after jumping from his tree-fort on a dare.

Now, wake in a cold sweat
as winter rain beats the sill—

reach and gently find the hip
covered in blankets, near enough.

Imagine, if you will,
these factories of cope,

these pillars on the horizon,
none so fixed as the fountain.

None so affirming as the allowance
of rapture as unifying constant.

Four.

**EARTHMOVER**

## Mad Dog's Act of Extended Departure

Farewell to nighttime, Sinatra, and blueberry wine.
       *Let's give your neighbors something to talk about.*
I understand the need for a hot meal, but nothing tastes good
with a burnt tongue. Can you taste the allegory?
                  How do you find yourself
in the back of a cab at 3am with an elf on your lap
kissing your mouth and ear, tasting alternately
of brandy, nutmeg and sour nog? Aside from the Santa's
Little Helper cap, could you pick her from a crowd?
Probably not. Nearly dawn and I go out to the porch
for a Lucky Strike. I don't smoke but I wish I did—
at least then I'd have an excuse for standing on the porch
listening to motors, calculating the weight of the good deeds
it will take to outweigh the night prior. The priory of sion—
            was that a real thing? It wasn't
but it seemed that way. Sangreal: Seemed real.
And a radish carved to look like a rose turning out
looks instead like a fist turning in, choking itself.

Farewell to the New Year, it's nearly time. I've resigned
to never be famous, eternal relevance will do.
                      11:00 am on a Tuesday
and you wish you were a church goer 'cause today you do
and you put what's been broken by cab fare in the basket
and who the hell do you think you're talking to?
Was it you who was speaking of sovereignty? If so, have you
found what you're after? Can you call her by name?
Can you break her into pieces on the altar?

## JIM DAVIS

Farewell to the good old days of nothing but future.
Farewell to mad dogs moaning, small squirrels lost
in streets paved with smashed-squirrels.
Another thing: Find yourself a Chicken Shawarma, shower,
then go behind the dumpster and puke.

That's it. You've done it again. Call it a night, she said
but you wouldn't listen. Step out on the porch for a smoke ...
      *Ahem*. City, unzip your dress, I've been waiting for you.

**EARTHMOVER**

## Acrostic Variation

*One*

Every fifteenth finger of Wild Turkey shoots
Time in the heart.
I am 23, no, 24, ridding myself of fish tacos & whiskey & I
Think of you, blindly, eyes wretched shut, think
Of drawing lace curtain across a window's breath,
You & the smooth brine of ocean air, forgetting.
I use my sleeve to wipe my chin, hail a taxi, spill in &
Throw my phone out the window, where it floats
Up into the blue fading desires of night; pulverized by dawn.

*Two*

Every finger-thick link in the chain mirrors
Time in the worst way: locked & fated: if only
I were a birthday cake delivered to a prison …
Think of the chisels I could hide!
Of the afterlife, I wonder, the fraternity of old souls—
*You never stumble through equivocation—*
I struggle with chisels, sugar-frosted & clumsy, I
Throw my hands in the air. Breathe easy. There are moments
Up here in the hill-tower when I'd rather sit than fall.

**JIM DAVIS**

## New Kid Tries to Fill Big Shoes
*a Superboy semi-cento*

Don't get up, hairballs—I can let myself in.

Red & Blue gumption: Steel hand. Glass jaw.
                It figures.
Come to think of it ... the volume was way up
on Easy Street. I could'a missed a few things.

Your body on the small motorized bicycle makes me delirious.
Your purple hair is a preposition, is connective tissue
before you make a stand. Preposit. Presuppose and you will
amalgam us an ass. In the act of proposing you should take
a knee in order to fortify your stance. See also: predicament.

The table is giving us trouble, so low, and I'm so damn high
off genetic predisposing, sweat beads breathe in superclouded
sunbeams blasting my veins with coffee I want everything
to collapse in clean, satiated exhaustion. Mark Twain
maybe wrote with a wag of dry grass in his teeth, or a corncob

pipe—that's a different jungle, the prairie, this is concrete—
when you fall here you don't sink or bury, you splatter.
Please don't die before I do, please don't never die.
Paul Celan reorders clean trousers in the sink.
                              Superlinguist.
      Sitting in the sun, belt buckle
      so hot when she spits on it, it sizzles.

## EARTHMOVER

You're a slow curtain, I say, a momentary lapse. She bends over
to unlace red sandals roped up her calf, slip into something
quick, before someone needs to use the phone booth.
No way I'd let anyone kill a beautiful babe like you!

Me—I got a never-ending battle with my name on it.

## JIM DAVIS

## Orchestra

I tried the outdoors once, they didn't suit me.
You said it was late November and that shouldn't count.
But it counts, of course it does.
I'm looking out the window now. And it's fine.
The trees are pulled apart by wind, yellow and failing.
The tide tongues the coast and recedes.
The season is over. The woman at the table in my periphery
unties the scarf around her neck and lets it fall.
I pick it up and hand it to her. Then I go back
to the world beyond the window. Tonight, she will
think about me. You can see her scars,
the lighting so dramatic. The empty cadence of gears
ticking in her wrist watch become a metronome,
I tap my feet to it. Thin hands vibrate, become
a conductor's wand, twitching before the pit
of string and brass. Every string is silk and strong,
together they web, together trapped. Against the fence,
a collection of fallen leaves, their piles interrupted
by soda cans, empty bags, abrupt roots and arms
of severed hedges, woven through the steel web of chain-link.
I breathe against the glass and write a message in the fog.
Beneath her seat is a brown paper package wrapped in string.
In the pot-belly stove down the road, leaves are burning.
Why would anyone leave the dry inviting heat of home?
The room pulses with awful, expanding silence: a chorus
that dips and rises into blades wiping a windshield,
bathes in crescendos to the cadence of my tapping feet.

**EARTHMOVER**

## Understanding the Nature of the Desert

I drew a map in the sand with a stick.
Face stung by exposure, vultures hover over
like water circling the drain. The milk jug
had been buried in the garden, filled
with a few copper coins, a Polaroid,
and an early attempt at writing: a letter
to my future self that begins: *Hello, if you are alive.*
I dust away the crumbs of blue-corn chips and drink
from a cactus branch. I drink from an aloe stalk,
drink one thousand tart cherries, pressed and bled.
Wind wipes away the map. The dunes lift and set
like waves. I am grateful for warmth, grateful
for conversation. I have read the Outsiders
now that I am too old for the Outsiders, old enough
to appreciate it. I have fallen on my sword.
I drew a picture, called it Black: My Suicide.
Stopped by the light off the dune, I envision myself
as a painter. I have to squint. The wind is blinding.
As for the sword, it strikes as it ought to.
A fig beetle rises from its burrow and scuttles
through the desert, to no place particular.

## Another Retreat

Lydia was her name, he thinks, she lived
off Evergreen, made her money waiting
tables, spent her days learning the names
and inauguration order of the presidents.
Vegan, she might have been, she made him
leave his shoes at the door, pet the cat.
He curled his toes to cure the smell of feet.
She's down the road from a Russian bathhouse,
shut down, boarded. The hallway of her building
had a slight sewer smell, which you'll get
used to, she said. Her neighbors have a dog,
he noticed. I think you know more than you say
you know, more than you let on. Her cheeks
glowing red, teeth red and dull from cheap
merlot, this song, she said, you know it, don't
you? He did, fingers already pressing chords
into an imaginary neck, strumming the rhythm
of the song she hoped to show him. It played
again on the radio beside her bed, to drown
the noise they made. The cat hopped up
where they lay and breathed heavy, sweating
slightly. He'd eaten an ahi tuna sandwich, seared
and slathered with aioli, the only meat on the menu
at the vegan eatery. He pushed the cat aside
and dressed, blaming his allergies. He left.
On the blue carpet in her room, a book of presidents
open to the 25th page, the bushy eyebrows of William
McKinley, concerned, most likely, with the Treaty
of Paris, which had Spanish implications, she explained
to the empty intersections of wall, as an old song played
slowly, and a car roared to life in the street.

**EARTHMOVER**

## Two Bears Fighting on an Alaskan Beach

One of them dumps.
This is not an acrostic, though it behaves like
Forgetting. Sky-scraping terrors glittering
Like fish scales on the dock of an afternoon.
Enwreathed in thick fog like a robe around the thickness
Of grizzly necks and shoulders. Thinking of this
Many years later, tired, when even the yogurt encrusted
Spoon seems relevant. Upside down, the buildings of the city
Escape fire, taste like clove cigarettes, kindle memories of two huge
Grizzlies fighting on an Alaskan beach. One dumps.
In the eighteen wheeler transporting oranges or bundles of pot
Under the guise of oranges, the driver taps ash, renders
The cherry of his cigarette useless. Upside down
The terrible buildings look like children
Tipped back on a tire swing, like a maple tree
Clinging desperately to earth. Natural savagery
erupted. As it tends to.
Tire swinging from an effervescent shoelace.
The streets are paved with bloodlust like a beach, although
What's interesting is not the fighting of the bears, but the way
Their fight has enwreathed itself into the day, non-separating
Like salt come solution. Dear Tropicana, you cannot stick a straw
Through the skin and pith of any worthy fruit.
What's happened to the coding of ambivalence, the cadre of grizzlies
Stealing pic-a-nic baskets, stealing salmon from their moments
Of inspired flight; encoding hyper-aggression ... what next?
Aggression again, all it every was—what's next is universal.

This is not an acrostic, I said—in being what it truly is, it is barely itself.

## JIM DAVIS

## The Pigeons Lean-Out and Come in Swarms

Smudge of selfness on the city
in April as it thaws.

The car that sat all winter
refusing to turn over
has sprouted legs
opened its mouth like a yawn.

You will hear Chicago now
in the song-like cadence of birds

that is not at once a song, and the smell
of dog turds relaxing. If one is destined
to die with boots on, it is time
to consider sandals

and if pudgy, stumped toes
and meaty hooves impede you, think of this:

even bananas are said to make you fat, and apples
and the skinner you are on your death bed, the sadder
your loved ones will be—such a dilemma is only so
in the company of time, outside of it, or stacked

on a hill of beans looking down into itself.

And the pigeons once again descend upon the city
leaner now and bright with hope, leaving white-
scat droppings to scar the fountain ledge.

The whistling city shrugs its shoulders, hikes up its dress,
and spreads its chubby legs, slick with new humidity.

**EARTHMOVER**

## Waiting Out Traffic After Gas and Groceries

Sitting outdoors at the organic grocer, bits of sweet
potato flecked in my chin stubble, a kind mid-June
wind picks up what's grown nearby, wafting.
                              Geranium? White ivy?
Anyway, Dear Diary, it's time—no—dear underside
of a recycled paper plate, here's what I believe:

When the first layers of rain press down, they bring creamy
musked air, forcing smog like a French Press from above
the city, glinting cool melons in a crate.
Spent, stewing in a time-stop, hiccough in the milieu
like green-brown cow patties in a field: stagnant luxury.
If you've ever seen the well you know what comes forth

like a storm. Two boys skating a cart. Quick cat across
the parking lot. Two women fight as they carry paper
bags to the car—one can only see in tigers, the other
in alewife, small stinking fish washed up
on the blackfly shore. Soon I'll give up on my moment,
stack thin books of poetry and set them on my package

of Lemon Zest Pizelles, greek yogurt, guacamole. Oh Dear
paper plate, tonight Tony Parker, I mean tonight Manu Ginobli
will float a giant killer over the overpaid behemoth
from Houston. Two books in the bag. Starlings have nested
and any mention is a conjure of York's blessed murmuration.
He's gone too. I say this now to tell you

that the day began with someone's being gone. Their gone-
ness heightened by a song whose chords I'm unwilling to learn:

## JIM DAVIS

*If you call me I won't be home, I'm hiding from the kingdom come*
*...*
Inspiration is funny thing: a man with a sore neck dreamed
of black spores as he deprived himself of sleep, dreamed
of himself as a perched gargoyle swatting flies, began to dream

in herbs, then, for weeks, woke with the most divine russet potato
dusting you'd ever want to try. Secret blend, oil, then bake. Woke
with a spectacular turkey rub and a raging hard-on.
That was then, now the empire of this patio trembles
as a plane picks up speed, closes the distance.
*This is why hell is underground* ... After this, I'll spit my lips into

a soup of potato, scallion, human flesh and a pint of heavy cream.
Silver platter, roasted game bird, expertly seasoned.
Melons in a bowl after the melon baller. I wonder
where that cat went. I wonder what the woman with the tiger
tongue tasted, since she couldn't eat meat. I should have
gone to the olive bar. I should have learned another song to play

since they asked for the one I won't. Since I already know
what happened to the boys. Flicker of time-space watching
two flies plaiting paths from the turkey to the bulb. Sprout.

If this is it and nothing more, the point must have been planted.

**EARTHMOVER**

## Dig

It is not so sweet to be anything
other than a hasped fissure
of night and day. The engine
ticks and cools and you lean to kiss
over the arm rest. We'd lie in the grass
beyond the softball fields, combing
ourselves for promise, unable
to see sniggers shaking the bush.
The night went the way of fire,
tonguing us; the pole was dug
into the soft ground, it bent;
the line quivered, thin and taught;
we pulled the blanket to our chins.
I find this morning to be the perfect burn
of orange and red in the trees.
Gills flare, soft and warm.
Wet scales shudder at the moon.
I will find the same plot of land
near the fields, split the heavy earth
and lift it with a spade. I will dig
and decide, this is a good enough grave,
or at least it will be, at least it might.
Cheast heaving, breath rising as steam.
I lean against the handle of the blade.
The morning will save me.
The mug will warm my hands.

## Agoraphobic

In the pasture, a boy hangs upside down
from an oak-limb, shaking acorns to see
the world. On paper its fury is striking,
the up-skirt, dazzling. When do you put the pen down
and get serious? I am no more human than fire
is split logs, is crackling leaves, dried pinecones
spitting luminescence on wet, shadowed grass.
                    I too am warm.
You drape a blanket across my knees. Again
with the oak trees. Leave the cabin, wander,
understand that arriving on time is secondary
to depth of movement, to quality of interaction.
Where are all the children? You ask, as if you had
no perception of roads and their teeth, of the schoolyard
and its mighty stinger. Dementors hug the corners,
always under streetlamps, the dumpsters in the alley
too dramatic. But if you must know, the children are
in the pasture, upside down, to see the flowing river
from a different angle:
                    howling unearthly, they unzip the mudbank
and pull toads from it, from the river bed, in a gray cloud
of mosquito; they paddle, skin breaking into rash, tiny
bumps rising like tide beneath the bridge, they lie
back in the canoe to clear it, stare at the spiders weaving
the bridge's planked underside, sprinting to secure
a mosquito for dinner. A toad expands and croaks
in one's pocket as they float. He'll grab the boat walls, rock
and threaten to tip the lot, until the kind sun finds feet, legs, heads
and they sit up, paddle again. The spider howls unearthly, unzips
the body he has wrapped and sucks it dry.
                    The river is sweet. Cup hands, drink.

**EARTHMOVER**

## Earning Stripes in the Cellar

Kicking rocks into a black lake
        of swans that spread and lift, shade
and shower us with black, baptismal wind.
        I have wasted hours pining at the window,

igniting evergreens, the pulsing white lines
        that weight their arms. I dig through the needles
molting slowly, and the gray snow that begs.
        Shaken from sleep, I claw at the song on the radio,

aching for refrain. The self-destructive art
        of putting words to moments, ideas, poetics—
where words inherently fail. In the dark
        I mapped out your body for the first time,

returned frequently. Stacked pin oak, post oak
        limbs to dry, shackled the roof to the sky.
If you'd let me, I'd begin again. I'd spend a lifetime
        picking chords to the same song. And to tell you

the truth, it wouldn't matter. I wake up shaking.
        I drink till it's appropriate, shake the guitar
for quarters. It was something with rhythm, I recall,
        something you didn't much care for, after all.

Still, when it scratches through the speakers
        as you drive through the night and its white,
pulsing highways, you adjust the volume,
        stare like a stone drunk, tap your fingers

                as the black lake stains your toes.

### JIM DAVIS

## The Dripping Faucet

They said he was a good soldier,
a constant in the boy scout reserves, strapping
frasier firs to station wagon rooftops.
When he grew, the man at the newsstand said
*Boy, you know how to live!*
Assuming he would snack on crackers and cheese
that night. Most nights. There is crippling efficiency
in laundry and dishes and other such things.
In '84, Reagan threw fat fistfuls of funding
at Walter Mondale, told him to screw himself.
Of course, there was more then than there is now.
And somehow the mystery brought everyone closer.
Alone on the beach, he jabs his cocktail umbrella
into tiny ice cube islands, hoping they will sink,
melt, and make his drink more bearable.
He sees a woman tucking an auburn tress behind her ear,
she twirls gum and pops it with her mouth.
He is barebacked on the lawn,
stirring slightly, hoping for the promised wind.
Damn you, Augustine, for questioning yourself.
Damn you, Springtime, and all your ruined cities.
Damn this heat and our patchwork lives.
The faucet dripping, the shrapnel of confetti
from a ticker tape parade sticking to the sink.
Damn the whiskers on the canvas-come-basin.
Explain why we need so many deadsoldiers,
and how it ever seemed like a good idea.
From the tap, expanding beads,
the fullest among them at the lip of the drain.

## EARTHMOVER

with the bill, and I still have to be at work. To think
that another in the same situation might carve
his name, or near directions, in unrecognizable script
or dip his fingers into a sweet light coffee to stir
the cream and save the fly and slowly sip what's left
past staining teeth and souring tongue, close his eyes
and breathe the subtleties of therapeutic rewiring, muted
wail of a train, wherein whose wake he once set down
some Swedish fish, a plastic comb, his first handful of coins.

## JIM DAVIS

## Stallion Left for Dead

Turn your face to the whispering ghost-horse
giving away the tricks of the trade: how to
pull a sword from stone (the secret lies
in the grip: aim the fusion of thumb and index knuckle
at your dominant shoulder). He's eating tiger-
lilies, pulling up clover with his chisel-
sized teeth and loose horse lips, which tell
of two ships sunk in the harbor, they were
tethered together when one was struck
by lightning, took three days to sink, drug
the other with it, it wasn't until the ice melted
anyone noticed they were gone—all winter
the thin ice-layer whispered with undercurrent—
they all assumed the two were still out there
talking in low, hushed voices, like the couple
outside on the patio, cursing each other's jealousy
between cigarettes. Don't get a ghost-horse drunk,
he'll tell you stories of his high school baseball team—
district champs. I could fly, boy, he'll say, before
getting into the story of a mare: *what for
such plaitlets come undone, unto their pining master ...*
(he can really be an ass sometimes). His owner
carved and grilled a sowbelly, one sunny afternoon
with the dry-rub-recipe-for-disaster peppered
on ribeyes. He'll explain how that mare left him
for a living horse. He'll give you the answer
to the wonder of warm summer breeze: a ghost-horse whinny,
telling of the farmer who put him down, one bolt to the skull
as he retreated into the corner of the pen. Smell of hay
and shit. And the farmer, when he was done with it, sent the stable-
boy in after, while he went back to work, carving God
from hard bars of soap, rocking slowly on the porch.

**EARTHMOVER**

## Semiotics of Settling

The many gold rings she removes
and sets on the bedside table, nibbling at the quicks
of her fingernails, hair pulled back with a tie, sheer
black leggings despite the cold. Cedar Key
Florida makes a nice vintage
t-shirt, which Maribel folds
at the Laundromat on South Street. In the receding
lake of what's important/what's ignored
cigarette smoking is big, and if you sneeze
                into your hands
        I will begin to hold you under. We will
say, *that's what people like us do—*
take ski vacations in Park City, Sun Valley,
places like that—and I knew
exactly what I meant, though I'm not sure
anyone else did, so I said it again
a little louder and did a little dance.
*You really cut to the hyponychium*, she said,
which is the etymological root
of a nail's quick: it's what's left alive
after the dead nail sprouts. I was 29
when I first learned to fold a pair of pants.
After the mid-day applause
I practiced Spanish on the guitar,
ran with the collarless cats
three times through the alley,
one time shook it on the porch.
Gold, gold, and gold moreover.
Electrified by static. The quiver

## JIM DAVIS

of the bed table as the earth shakes,
as we are showered in gold—
it's our drowning that will have to be
enough, which, compared to the symbol
for choking, will seems quite fluid and serene.

## The Dance of a Wasp

The dance of a wasp
beside the body of another wasp.
He cried hard then slept.
When he woke there was only one wasp left,
the dead one. Less sad without.
Ribbons of blood, then the band plays.
Days on a yellow couch. The march forgotten.
The tree ribs will blossom with prompting.
Summer. The hard wings of beetles
tapping at the lamp. Getting fat
for good reason. A schoolboy in a church collar
kicks real-estate signs, karate chops low branches.
At lunch, a light brush of oil to cauterize the bun.
Tar coating the oval where a tree branch once was
something so essential to this life: denial,
optimism, transcendence. Wishes on every eyelash,
on every eleven-eleven, to be happy again.
The only certainty the buzzing expectation
that at one point, he was.

Five.

**EARTHMOVER**

## Article Quick

Raven on the fencepost.
                         I learned young
what not to expect, riven and sewn
back with maudlin thread.
                    Riding home through well-worn
         tracks of winter, slightly drunk—
these days I share quite fewer cabs, it seems
I hardly remember when I don't, which is
not promising for either of us, whoever you are
                           I'm sorry


I didn't clean up after—how could I have known
I'd be meeting and forgetting you so soon? You, the crest
and flutter of a bed sheet, beige and clean, then gone.

Lightning, char, seeds of doubt
                        sprouting in the ash.

The more one writes of indiscretion, the less likely it is
        to be forgiven. Object permanence
or abstract resonance? Abject subsequence like catching
mist in a butterfly net. And the hollow feeling is less
                       for a moment
like the brown cow lost on the shaded hill-shoulder, held
by tufts of grass and clover—even that quadri-chambered
creature understands the being of somewhere just
        beyond the ridge, where a bevy of sound
ambles off to a barn of weathered foxtail pine, penned
and dry. Blackbirds at the body of a small brown fox.

## JIM DAVIS

Smell of burning leaves. Sound of brittle hay
flattening. A thick maple stool in the corner of the stall.

So much to say of expectation. Fall hardens into winter.
Then spring. And the muted sound of freight horns, wary.

And the quick flash of smoke from fire cleansing prairie.

**EARTHMOVER**

# Mint Sauce and the Tongue of Gerald Stern

Shawl, said the man with an angora plaited pattern
wrapped around his neck, it shall be the wet blanket
of what we extinguish, the lamb of electric fire, insofar
as the lamb will live alone in roaring virtue, he says,
in the lust it perpetuates and fears. Stuck
in the gum of an outdoor table, on the last agreeable
afternoon, the assumed sex of a red speckled beetle.
In streets of consciousness, these bald valleys
of mind, clear, although it is predicted
winter will be ornery, especially in the morning—
our only hope the spastic hum of the plow, to lighten
the canals of our knowing—clean sheets cannot be
likely. Drum of cold water from the rust encrusted tap.
I said it once before and meant it: in a still life,
when pressed hard enough, anything can kill, the butter knife
erect in a cluster of dirty dishes, is no exception.
Billy Eckstine draining conversation from the moment.
Driving home from the war, I noticed an opossum, he said
on the side of the road. He camped there for days, every morning
he was bigger, full of bloat, expanding in his pity
until the rains came, followed by a glass of wine, pad of butter
in the shape of a crouching lamb, the shank of inspiration,
roasted, as we devour the prodigy of mint preserve.
He turned down the beds and did the laundry.
He opened the window when the sauce went off.
He sliced the roasted lamb as if it were the lard of life.

# JIM DAVIS

## Hoarse

He walked all day through the forest, unaware of the leak
in what he called his sweet-sack, a small paper bag of sugar
and hard candies, peppered with grit from his travel:
bits of dry oak leaf, cinnamon, some thyme. Later
he came upon a badger in the thicket, as he approached
its comical bark startled him. He has heard that if a badger bites
it will not release before defusing the threat, so you are
supposed to snap a twig in your hands and scream
like a bone has broken. He dips into the sack, sprinkles
a handful over a pile of red leaves. He engages the badger
in conversation: What was the name of the child whose wings
melted after a day in the sun – or was it night, wax dripping
by the blaze of the hearth? Either way, he was taken
by wind coming in from St. Paul, a strong nor'wester that swept him
clear across Ohio, until he got hung up in a briar near Charleston.
That's coal mining country, said the man begging for sugar
door to door in Muskingum county. What was his name? Horace?
Anyway, said the man to the badger, my father spent all day working
on a cracked sewer main. He could play the acoustic guitar,
Burl Ives, given the season, mostly love songs
that told of nothing more than the way she was: a dry reflection
of something wet: blood, maybe, or wine. She told him once
that horseradish hollandaise was meant to be drizzled over Charleston
crab cakes and there was no exception. She screamed
when the neighbor's Palomino Quarter Horse jumped the fence
and ate the pride of her garden, pulled full sunflower blooms from stalks.
Horace was his name, after the soldier-poet who removed his helmet
which was carved and painted like a falcon, set it on the table
and took her small hands into his own. Now that the sewer caps

## EARTHMOVER

are soldered on and the caves in the quarry are bouldered-over
you can sprinkle some of this into your tea with milk.
How can the crows call so crudely without losing their voices,
he wondered, holding the stare of the badger in the thicket.
What matters is that, without entry, notes return
to the origin, the instrument of their making. Three pups
poked out their tiny faces. What matters now is that sweet
bag of sugar is almost empty, and there's no reason to yell
once your voice is lost forever, once the rain washes away
the sweet lines of your journey.

**JIM DAVIS**

## The Best Poem I Have Ever Written

Each morning, well, on the mornings I wake
in time to find the dawn beginning to beat
the mild rhythm of early summer, I read and take notes
and read and finally write what is, daily, the best poem I have

ever written. Sound of snoring for the other room. The dog
is lying in a patch of sun and I am tired of writing
about her death before she has died. I will lie
next to her, later, once I've written the best poem I have

ever written, she's the only one whom I can nuzzle up to
with a combination of coffee and morning breath. There is struggle
on days like today, to leave the Canada goose figurine
standing proud beneath the side table—where a photograph

of my grandmother touching the shoulder of her mother
in the only manner those chubby digits would have been able, gently
yellows in its frame—unacknowledged, that goose who was hers,
saved from the vacation home on a Wisconsin lake, before it was sold

and remodeled into, so I've been told, something worse—not quite
what we were used to. And it's possible, of course, that although
winds have spread umbrellas of dandelion seed to the ends of the yard,
that this is not the best poem ever written, but the best poem I have

to tell. Anything that crosses my path in growing warmth is worthy:
the flowering tree surrendering to standard green, thickening
with the season, the shudder of a mockingbird bathing in dust,
and that Canada goose, without whom this would be a poem

## EARTHMOVER

like any other—carved of heavy black walnut, hand painted,
every feather featuring the added texture of wood grain,
the downturned tail, the shut beak, and that long, ringable neck—
which belonged to my grandmother. I wonder if she,

in her yellowing pose, was asked to place her tiny hand
upon her mother's shoulder, or if the human grace within
drew its tender handle on the moment. It's not the same grace
which led her to serve the public, donate a lifetime

in schools of the blind, or find herself, on similar mornings
writing reflections in the margins of French-impressionist texts.
No, it's far simpler than that—closer, perhaps, to the impulse
of a man with a chisel and brush, to create. Wonder of a child:

a touch, and the slight upturned corner of a smile just like mine.

# JIM DAVIS

## Crawl Back After

Arms pinned back, he barely spoke
to those knuckles but they answered, just ask
the split incisor, his cracked rabbit tooth –
now, when he flosses he saves it for last.

In bed, the most generous, grateful prose is written
which is to say, the most sincere. She, who has
already taken back what she could, sulks and slumps
in a fitful cab, wind howling through the half-window

like a bomb-cloud skimming skyscraper tips: empty
with anticipation. She spins silently at the light, before the old
magnolia drops its petals. One flutters in and lands on her lap
like a snowflake, exceptional, matchless and steady, not melting

but breathing above her knee, which she slips between the pages
of a magazine. He, at the same time, was pissing in a trash can,
tugging at a smoke until he could barely breathe. Dizzy, he tipped
the can and cracked his head on the sink. She whirled and rolled

herself into a knot that night, a dance written in a dead language:
the approach of a kingfisher diving. When he returned he discovered
they'd shut off the heat, added layers with a bottle of wine.
He stayed up late reading a Dictionary of Theories,

but could not steady the lines on the page. He spent an hour painting
and remembered days he would sing the shower clean.
In the morning, he'll attempt to glue the pieces of vase. He'll fold
laundry to the drama of some foreign soap opera, understanding

## EARTHMOVER

the similarities, save the hangover, to a high school football game:
twelve minutes per quarter. He'll squander an afternoon
composed by Hans Zimmer, which he shall refer to
as the Day of Black Smoke, Fire, and Back Pain.

About the floss, he saves the cracked tooth for last
since the line frays, ruined like most once they touch.
She admires the fine writing of dusk and all the subtleties
of the year dislodged, or gently dismembered.

# JIM DAVIS

## Return to Alma Mater: Napping Behind the Library Stacks

I am stirred by whispers from the other side
of the shelves: two students reading spines
in the half-conscious squint of June, otherwise,
the library rests, quiet as I imagine Pompeii
swallowed by six meters of ash must be, after ash

has strangled sound. Pompeii, they whisper,
printed in gold on the thick red length of a guided tour, in pictures.
Dust motes in the sun cutting across the sill, the stacks, two chairs
I've pressed together, to nap. As they shuffle off, I linger in the novelty
of my position: an arm chair, hidden behind the atlas bank.

Although there is no great significance
to my return, there is, if nothing else, a view
of the fire escape turning over itself
along the brick face of a place I used to live. Barely a scar
of sunlight now, as I recall the night, the catholic moon

above my current position, from the opposite view.
I stepped out onto the grated landing
on a Saturday, that first week of school,
and noticed a quiet room across the grounds
where someone had left a light on, somehow aware

of the great nostalgia to come. Pre-nostalgia, if there was
such a thing—I would be, rather, I have always been
wading through its late waves, the legs of my pants cuffed
above the knee, wondering at the cool nothingness
of the water, squinting in the glow of the new evening,

## EARTHMOVER

of all its blinking stars. There's a book split on my lap
with notes penciled in the margin: *suffering is hardly unique*, it says,
so I shut the book, softly. Loneliness, contemplative blues
thump across generations—a rhythm been beat
into campus pathways for years, and years to come.

Another note: *I want to know less and understand more*, it says. Hum
of a vacuum is not enough to drown the muted sound of freight horns
in the distance. I take one final trip to the atlas
section, tilt a few spines. I find, upon looking through spaces created
by missing text, through and out the window, across the lawn, holding
on

to the fire escape with white knuckles, frozen
like the final pose of Romans buried by ash,
                                    some familiar figure staring back.

## JIM DAVIS

## Defining History

Driving along the carved arteries
that slice through mountains like sides of beef
witness to the braille of their interior flesh, marbled

shelves of rust, themselves, it seems, do gently rustle,
turnover at daybreak, sleeping giants as they are, forms
under a blanket of Appalachian Flora—alive, despite

their utter facelessness. There is comfort to be found
in anonymity. So goes the journey to the place of our making,
the eastern port where smaller, uglier versions of ourselves—

assuming precision within photography of the time—
first touched ground after weeks against the urging sea,
back and forth, back and forth with their decisions, pitching

half-digested breakfast over the hull. Days go by. Years.
And here's what it's been whittled down to: he is sitting indoors,
reading about the most appropriate way to cure an infant

stung by a scorpion: suck and spit, suck and spit, press
a poultice of red mashed potato and tobacco resin at the entry—
when a woman walks past, and he's sure she is in love with him.

It's eleven degrees today, and windy, so it's a feeling
she might never know. However, and he has this
on good word, come down from the mountain giants,

she stays awake at night, half awake, in and out of dream,
thinking of the many times she has walked past him
carving into arteries of what she's missed.

## Blizzard

Prating drool of night announces
commandments for the birds. Who have
left a tremble in electric branches.

Parked plows breathe in musked anticipation—
hunger for snow drift that swallows houses whole.
In case you are able to hear above the blizzard,

I have been saving my last words.
I leave my boots at the door and do not bother
with the lights. Static bulbs needs relief.

There is no player piano, no pre-ordained
songs—on the table there are shells, no yolk,
cracked orange peel without the meat of the rind.

On the coral wall at my bedside, mosaic
shadow of a window fan. Yellow umbrella
from the gaslight streetlamp carves features

for a man holding a knife in his teeth,
flipping a coin and humming some old navy song
about roses and whiskey, gulls and gathered grain.

Frightened and alone after floating an ocean
of insomnia, years of counting sheep,
a blanket quiet falls upon me

like the muted snow of the lawn
forgiving silent nights, losing
fingers to the black frost morning.

## JIM DAVIS

## Sediment

Her brow grooves, so fiercely
engaged in her studies, a knit cap
is pulled to her eyes which soften
as a line of children pass on a string.
Their steps are quick and clumsy.
On my quivering palm, I wonder
at the blue light that hisses beneath
the open book—I should mention that
I have spent the past year learning to read & write.
I'm telling you, that sibilance of hers
is hypnotic, I wear it like a gown,
or a knit cap pulled to my eyes.
I breathe it and allow the gray smoke of it
to bend like the blanket broken over her
legs, until all the light around me
dims to ash. I spend the rest of the day
unwilling to forsake my chair for fuel.
She has mapped out the seasons
on blue-flake paper. And for the rain,
the soap smell has left us. The streets
are frothing. The line is broken,
the children splash and play. Their clumsy
steps scribbled in sheets of downpour.
Footsteps in the ash smoothed over
by the tide. The moon soothes quiet
the mews and what once was a garden
of cabbage and snapdragons. Their scent,
intoxicating, though not so much as before
the rain, when the blue light covered everything.

**EARTHMOVER**

## In a Coffee Shop in the Plaza on Weed Street

Between mouthfuls of wheat bagel drowned in cream cheese,
a small white bead perched in the stubble of aspiring moustache,
he told me about his drive home to the suburbs
for Christmas—he declared "You can't write about this, Christmas
has become the farthest thing from 'poetic.'" He went into particulars
of the drive: unseasonable warmth, sunlight, geese, snow or no snow,
bent fluorescent tubes and blinking bulbs patiently awaiting night.
For a while I was distracted by a man at the table by the bathroom,
busy with razorblades, nub pencil perched sentry-like near the crown
of his skull behind his ear. A spinning compass needle, blue gridded paper,
involved entirely with a solitary task. " … sickly interpretation of intent … "
In the corner near the door, a small child's hand held by a mother,
speaking softly like old friends. A boy with a soft brimmed cap, three scarves
layered and contra-patterned, divided by the strap of a messenger's pack
and a cup too large for his hands. He begins tapping two chapped fingers
to the beat of a tired song that everyone began to tap to. The magnificent swell
of a coffee shop tapping. We went on like this and cleaned our table and left.
Walking home, I noticed a set of couch cushions hidden behind a pillar
under the highway overpass. Wounded wreathes left in a vacant lot
where troop 19 had been selling trees. I recalled his story:

It was not until he left, 12:15am, once everyone had fallen to sleep
when he caught the eye of the tree, it being the only light of the room,
humming dutifully in what slight pine scent still lingered, unwrapped
boxes stacked among their own colorful rind. On the drive back
into the city, the earth seemed to rise and it rained and he began
to believe everything he'd heard, he began to worry that he had not
locked the door behind him—he told of the terrible images
he imagined, the plunder and murder, the lungfuls of smoke
that rose in his mind's eye, as fire drank up everything inside—

## JIM DAVIS

how the owl and deer would freeze in its warmth. He said,
setting the last bite of bagel into the basket, that he cried
for a few miles. It was late, there were no other cars on the road
and he went home to an empty apartment, set his keys on the table
and cinched the mouth of the trash, which had begun to smell.
He had his hood up, avoided puddles, and when he lifted the dumpster lid
two rats sat up on their hind legs, looking up at him like their god
had just opened the tin can of the sky to bathe them in light
of a flickering streetlamp. He didn't flinch, he said, he dropped
the sack of trash on top of them with a chirp and waft of sour air.
He heard a child crying in a garden apartment, then the hush of a mother.
The pepper trees were bare but supple, not yet brittle from cold, they reached
into the sky, he was certain, trying to peel back the clouds
at the aperture of star, the one star left in the growing manger of smog.

**EARTHMOVER**

# Golden

All morning staring at the falcon perched on a leather glove.
Deliberate repositioning. Talons like muted shotgun triggers
in crisp Chicago winter. The Golden Nugget challenges
the Golden Apple to a battle of tight-eyed breakfast spots.
The Nugget—across from Nikos' Gyros Stand, where Niko
employed Armando to slice the beef and lamb, Debbie to
sweep the floor, though she would be gone in summer, when
classes let out—offers 2 buttermilk pancakes, 2 extra-large eggs,
2 links of dry sausage and hash browns for $4.99 & a bottle
of wine, out the door. The Golden Apple, on the other hand,
is rumored to warm funnymen after they improvise second-
city assemblies – some big names, we're told. Across the street,
St. Alphonsus' Church, where he received communion,
admitted only forgivable sins, (he heard being mean to you sister
was worth the repetition of seven *Hail Marys* and one *Our Father*).
The Russian bell tower cathedrals have gone gray with time.
He scoffs at neglect, selfish dismissal of tennis shoes to the lamp line.
Repentance. The falcon drops for field mice & smaller birds. Coats
bled dry in bolls of what might be cotton. Repetition (sounds about
right) & repentance share the confines of oak chambers, polished
delivery. The bell tower's narrow corridors, tiles from the revolution-
ary mosaics in red and white, fall. Repetition, repetition, we were
to meet at the Golden Apple or Nugget, repentance ringing
from garden apartments. We were to meet at the fractal edge
of summer and nonexistence. We are distracted by nighthawks
slicing though whatever it is we've said. After all the acoustic
guitars have been cracked and bled of string, the hawks settle in
the golden bliss of satiation, that bliss of what we've emptied and held.

# JIM DAVIS

## Loam

*ping ping ping* as the pizza appears
on the counter—*ping ping* with the callous
palms of a brick oven pizza chef—here

& there, quarters are flicked & caught, slapped
on backs of sooty hands—pepperoni, okay—
mushroom-beef, chicken-waffle, *ping* macaroni

& white sand, silt clay—*ping*—why not
dig in the parkway, mug the beer & spill a little
at the fulcrum of our lives as we wait

for something greater. We have spent our time
burrowing, becoming night, tucked in
shadows, dancing in the corner of a brick oven.

When did we stop being our younger selves?
We nod our dirty heads, dozing, waiting
for the *ping* hot fresh long-awaited night to end.

**EARTHMOVER**

## Concern

His words were like exhausted steps
        in the woods over leaves when they're wet.
When every new sentence is insatiable
        burying its head in the host it has become.

Barley-corn tea steeping and smelling slightly of oak.
Baltimore, kimchi, periwinkle—once I wrote a poem
about Hibbard and lost it. Red maca root powder stirred
into my morning coffee. If you have ever spilled
into or out of a cab, then the moment
you're willing to give me is precious.
There is reason now to be concerned.

Scrap metal collector, dishwasher, pregnant daughter
with a too-small purple bra twisted atop the laundry,
given to the patches of dry grass coming up in fists
through resistant snow, prematurely thawing like a blanket
picked to pieces by moths. Paint the wrought iron white
if you don't mind. Pick your battles, stoke the fire and turn
the embers toward each other. Years from now, you'll see
that every bridge will have burned or rusted.

Strike a match and let it fledge into an ember. Set the glowing
tip upon the belly of the tick's engorging body, watch it's legs
twitching, imagine the surprise on its guilty feasting face.

# JIM DAVIS

## Story for a King

A glass of juice to begin with, handful of aspirin.
A moat of some sort. He's comparing seasons
to the moods of a day: cycles of promise
and heat. He's making notes in the dust of the sill.
Where were you when you invented your first
obsession? I'd bet it was April, or May—for me
wind tastes different whether beat
by a fan or the wings of a condor rising from a perch
in the Basel zoo. The little room where the Sun
Bear sits and diddles in the same air always,
so he expires. Conspiring, there is a newspaper article
wrapping my sandwich: two slices of brown meat, two slices
from a block of cheddar, leaves of butter
lettuce—slices and slices, and crumbs.
                                          October light
has a way of making you wonder if this day will ever come—
it does, says morning to the summer, you still have dusk
to fall. A little white truck idles
and I chases a wasp to the window—he stays and I let him
have a small lifetime. In the morning I will
take the paper from the steps, think of Basel (one of us was
still holding onto something) roll it into a swat
and end this for good. A number of birds have
changed their minds. The wind is mint, then cream
and day has broken, as it tends to
over the shin of a third strike. There are no caskets
for tiny bears. No tears. There never was a condor
and now Basel is on fire—the sergeant says, Move the earth
boys—we're out of water—move the earth and smother it.

**EARTHMOVER**

## Camera Obscura, Colorado

Certain struggles go unmoored, moving toward
the sovereign, sifting through plurals of dirt, the many
indices of earth. Like hogs sniffing out the cheapest

ways to sleep, stifle a sneeze or cauterize the hemorrhage
of what's unconnected, underdeveloped. If being is
determined by behavior we are all the under

of two rabbits rutting in the shadow of tomato vines.
I can be ruthless when I want to. These days
it's impossible not to write poetry in the fire-

web of grief, the soot line, ash-flack
heavy breathing of a brain stem massaged, please don't be
so fucking dramatic … it wasn't your son, not your brother,

only your small boulder to move, another in the wall
dividing lifetimes. Rotating the camera's focus to exhume
subtleties, small deposits of dirt, it's better to

drape the shade, remove the cap, depress the button, snap
the shutter, freeze in what could not possibly be
another love poem, not an elegy, not a word

of spring or fickle, pleasant weather, nothing of sheep skulls
in the meadow to ward away duende and welcome the duende
washing our man-skulls in the white water of Thunder Mountain

## JIM DAVIS

or Black Hawk Mountain—break me up why don't you,
tear your sleeves at the seams, angry with delight: curse
of unwilling discipline, cursed effervescence

of white water, algae boulders, resolving into streams.
When the weather turns and buds of another season begin,
the pictures of your laughter will have to be enough.

**EARTHMOVER**

## Sipping Tea at the Window, Colt Crosses Yard

Shadow is far from absence
of light. Every good painter can tell
of failures in observation. Ubiquitous clover, lonesome
foal, walking where a team of Appalachians once walked—
paths of beaten grass.

The glamour of what staggers
in the stable of what's gone
prides itself on the colt's budding conviction
and the yellow path it follows, breathing slightly: sprigs
of wild thyme and blue grass reaching, swaying, lithe—
daring the foal to beat them again. I was glad to
watch him cross, holding high his jaw and mane,
passing between patches of shadow and light
so naturally, it became difficult to tell the difference.

**EARTHMOVER**

# Notes

Ideas and italicized words in Trial are from the album *Are These Our Lives* by the Seattle-based hardcore band Trial.

One King Down borrows ideas and quotes from the Albany NY band of the same name.

There are two bands quoted in Earthmover: the band of the same name and a song of that name by the band Have a Nice Day.

Comanche is the name of General Custer's horse, who survived the infamous Battle of Little Bighorn.

In different mythologies, Dione is the Moon Goddess, a female Titan, beloved by Zeus, the mother of Aphrodite, and, in Stronger at the Start, the artist's name.

The quote that inspired Constant Is Rapt is a line from Kurt Vonnegut's *Sirens of Titan*, which occurred by way of an incidental page break.

Acrostic Variation is part of a project using the words within a phrase as the spine of an acrostic, rather than traditional letters/word. In this case, *Every time I think of you, I throw up*.

New Kid Tries to Fill Big Shoes quotes DC Comics' *Adventures of Superman No. 501: The Metropolis Kid Is Back!* referring to one of four characters claiming to be Superman after he has been killed by the monster Doomsday.

**EARTHMOVER**

# Acknowledgments

Thanks to Simone Muench, C Russell Price, Dan Fliegel, Anthony Opal, and Adam Lizakowski—voices of reason; John O'Connor, Eleni Makris, Monica Berlin; my family for their constant support; Abby and the tallies on the fridge; and Wilson.

Special thanks to the editors of the following journals, who first supported the work collected here, although it may have appeared under different titles and in slightly different forms:

*After Hours:* Signs
*Ann Arbor Review:* Listen to the Lions
*Avalon Literary Review:* Unearthing
*Bad Robot:* Acrostic Variations, The Best Poem I Have Ever Written
*Blinking Cursor:* Morgan Horse Silhouette
*Bluestem:* Dreaming of a Desert
*Blue Lake Review:* Report on a Ham Sandwich
*Boston Literary Magazine:* Defining History
*Circa Review:* Story for a King
*Contemporary American Voices:* Understanding the Nature of the Desert
*Danse Macabre:* Stallion Left for Dead
*the delinquent*: Birds on a Wire
*Dead Mule School of Southern Literature:* In a Coffee Shop in the Plaza on Weed Street
*Disingenuous Twaddle:* Big Sky Country
*Eunoia Review:* The Language of a City Changed Hands, What Was Said
*Eye on Life:* A Circle of Stones
*Fur-Lined Ghettos*: Contrition
*Heavy Hands Ink*: Chirp, Swallow
*Houston Literary Journal:* Promising Conclusion
*The Idiom:* Fire in the Bread Pan
*In Parenthesis:* Stronger at the Start
*Ishaan Literary Review:* Ordering Chilaquiles

## JIM DAVIS

*Magic Lantern Review:* Mad Dog's Act of Extended Departure
*Nether Poetry (Delhi):* The Last Tasmanian
*North Central Review:* Statue on the Green Near Water
*Other Poetry:* Earthmover
*Otoliths:* Golden, Mint Sauce and the Tongue of Gerald Stern
*Phantom Kangaroo:* Artemis: Diana, Again
*Poetry Quarterly:* Happening Upon a Golden Slipper in the Street
*Red River Review:* Truck Crossing a Bridge
*Requiem Magazine:* Another Persuasion
*Rufous City Review:* Another Retreat
*San Pedro River Review:* Past Kingdoms
*Subliminal Interiors:* Napping Behind the Library Stacks
*Town Creek Poetry:* Earning Stripes in the Cellar
*Whole Beast Rag:* Crawl Back After
*Wilderness House Literary Review:* Orchestra, Punctuated, Hoarse
*Willows Wept Review:* Sipping Tea at the Window, Colt Crosses Yard

Unearthing received honorable mention recognition in the *Avalon Literary Journal* Poetry Competition.
Circle of Stones received honorable mention recognition for the Eye on Life Poetry Prize.

Some of these poems previously appeared in the following chapbooks, at times under different titles and in slightly different forms:
*Seeds* (Kind of a Hurricane Press, 2013).
*Feel and Beat Again* (Mite Press, 2012)

**EARTHMOVER**

**Jim Davis** is a graduate of Knox College and an MFA candidate at Northwestern University. He lives, writes, and paints in Chicago, where he edits *North Chicago Review*. His work has appeared or is forthcoming in *Seneca Review, Adirondack Review, The Midwest Quarterly,* and *Contemporary American Voices*, among hundreds of other journals. Jim is the recipient of multiple Editor's Choice awards and a recent nomination for the *Best of the Net Anthology*. In addition to the arts, Jim is an international semi-professional football player.

www.jimdavispoetry.com

## Praise for *EARTHMOVER*:

*Jim Davis' poems skillfully negotiate a difficult but beautiful terrain, regions where "the stones tripped on / while turning soil are used to build walls." There is a keen eloquence that runs throughout Earthmover, a beauty even in "the whisper of dead things." Throughout, harsh reality means we confess, "amber poison you / have done me hard again." Yet Davis gives us a lasting, hard-earned solace, where a man admits painfully, "the pictures of your laughter will have to be enough." Earthmover is a highly commendable collection of poetry.*

—Jeffrey C Alfier, *San Pedro Review*

*The poems of Earthmover beautifully curate images of the physical and cognitive worlds, which Davis expertly weaves into lines that suggest a unique familiarity between reader and poet. His voice is one that pervades the psyche with a closeness that is comforting and engaging.*

—Phillipe Chatelain, *In Parentheses*

*Jim Davis'* Earthmover *is filled with his trademark layered imagery. Each poem weaves a vivid portrait of a moment, a thought, an observation. As you read, and then reread each piece you realized that what you're reading, what you're absorbing, what's unfolding before your eyes is a gentle gift: Jim Davis' vision of the world.*

—Valerie Rubino, *Avalon Literary Review*

## Other Titles by unbound CONTENT

*A Strange Frenzy*
By Dom Gabrielli

*Assumption*
By Jim Davis

*At Age Twenty*
By Maxwell Baumbach

*Before the Great Troubling*
*Our Locust Years*
By Corey Mesler

*Elegy*
By Raphaela Willington

*Inspiration 2 Smile*
By Nate Spears

*Painting Czeslawa Kwoka*
By Theresa Senato Edwards and Lori Schreiner

*Saltian*
By Alice Shapiro

*This is how honey runs*
*The Pomegranate Papers*
*Wednesday*
By Cassie Premo Steele

and many more.

Browse our bookshelf:
unboundcontent.com

www.ingramcontent.com/pod-product-compliance
Lightning Source LLC
Chambersburg PA
CBHW071719090426
42738CB00009B/1824